Victory and Woe

CENTENARY CLASSICS

Original publication dates of reprinted titles are given in brackets

Joseph Johnston, *Civil War in Ulster* (1913)
Darrel Figgis, *A Chronicle of Jails* (1917)
Ernie O'Malley, *Rising Out* (2007)
Padraig de Burca and John F. Boyle, *Free State or Republic?* (1922)
Mossie Harnett, *Victory and Woe* (2002)
P. S. O'Hegarty, *The Victory of Sinn Féin* (1924)

Victory and Woe

The West Limerick Brigade in the War of Independence

✦

MOSSIE HARNETT

*with a series introduction by Fearghal McGarry
and an introduction by James H. Joy*

UNIVERSITY COLLEGE DUBLIN PRESS
Preas Choláiste Ollscoile Bhaile Átha Cliath

First published in 2002 by
University College Dublin Press
Centenary Classics Edition 2015
© The Estate of Mossie Harnett 2015
Series Introduction © Fearghal McGarry 2015
Introduction © James H. Joy 2015

ISBN 978-1-906359-98-0
ISSN 2009-8073

University College Dublin Press
UCD Humanities Institute, Room H103
Belfield, Dublin 4
www.ucdpress.ie

CIP data available from the British Library

Typeset in Scotland in Ehrhardt by Ryan Shiels
Text design by Lyn Davies, Frome, Somerset, England
Printed in Dublin on acid-free paper
by SPRINT-print

CONTENTS

CENTENARY CLASSICS SERIES
INTRODUCTION
Fearghal McGarry

'The true history of a passionate period,' wrote P. S. O'Hegarty in *The Victory of Sinn Féin* in 1924, 'cannot be written by any contemporary. We are all too near it.' How does the revolutionary period appear from our present perspective, one hundred years after the Easter Rising? And, now that we have an abundance of 'the necessary documents and data' that O'Hegarty thought essential to write a balanced history, what do the voices of those who lived through this era have to tell us?

Although inevitably shaped by the period in which it was written, the historiography that has emerged over the past century has gradually transformed our understanding of the Irish revolution. The earliest accounts were mostly written by republicans. Popular memoirs by IRA leaders such as Dan Breen and Tom Barry, or the *Fighting Stories* recorded by Irish Volunteers throughout the country, often presented the conflict as a straightforward struggle between the Irish people and the malign forces of British imperialism. The Civil War was frequently overlooked, as were the perspectives of those who did not experience the preceding 'Four Glorious Years' as a period of liberation. This republican narrative was reinforced by school textbooks, as well as by State commemoration which centred on the sacrificial gesture of Easter 1916 rather than the more divisive violence that followed.

From the 1970s, when professional historians belatedly turned their attention to the period, more sophisticated and critical interpretations emerged. Local histories presented a more complex picture of the forces that shaped the conflict. Revisionist accounts emphasised social and political divisions rather than unity, and explored how factors other than patriotism, such as generational conflict, collective pressures and rising social frustrations, motivated many. Against the backdrop of the Northern Irish Troubles, the acrimonious debates that followed revealed a gulf between popular assumptions and scholarly perspectives.

Despite recent controversies centred on revolutionary violence in Cork, this gap has narrowed considerably, as is demonstrated by the transformation of attitudes to Irish soldiers in the Great War. The emergence of a more nuanced understanding of the past is also evidenced by the changing nature of State commemoration (even if this also reflects new imperatives resulting from the Good Friday Agreement, including a problematic tendency to understate past enmities). Notwithstanding criticism of aspects of the government's commemorative programme, the adoption of a 'decade of centenaries' incorporating the campaign for Home Rule, and Irish experiences of the Great War, alongside the War of Independence has enabled a more pluralistic approach than previous major commemorations. So too has the greater attention focused on the role of labour, women and campaigns for social reform.

Another positive development is the widening of access to contemporary sources through such projects as the digitisation of the Military Service Pensions Collection and the 1901–11 Census. Complementing these initiatives, UCD Press's new 'Centenary Classics' series makes available eye-witness accounts of key revolutionary episodes including the Ulster crisis; the aftermath of 1916;

the rise of Sinn Féin; the War of Independence; the Treaty split; and the Civil War. These provide first-hand perspectives on such topics as the significance of sectarian divisions; the impact of imprisonment on republicanism; the importance of popular mobilisation and guerrilla warfare; and the conflict's divisive legacy.

Although most historical controversies stemming from the revolutionary era focus on republican agency, Joseph Johnston's *Civil War in Ulster* reminds us how Ireland was plunged into crisis during a period when republicans exercised little influence. His account of the Home Rule crisis illustrates the role played by Ulster unionists, supported by powerful allies in Britain, in destabilising Ireland before the First World War. Ulster unionist defiance of Westminster, the formation of the Ulster Volunteer Force, and the establishment of a provisional government in Belfast exposed the limitations of the Liberals' Irish policy, not least its self-interested failure to reconcile the democratic demand of Irish nationalists for self-government with the right of Ulster's unionists to determine their own future. The divided loyalties of the British army in Ireland, exemplified by the Curragh mutiny of March 1914; the double standards of the police, seen in the contrasting responses to gun-running in Larne and Howth; and the undermining of the British Government by a Tory party whose incendiary rhetoric and support for armed resistance in Ulster verged on treason, contributed to the failure to achieve a peaceful settlement of the Irish question. Although sometimes interpreted as an irrational response to the Easter Rising, the collapse of popular support for Home Rule can only be understood within the wider context of the Ulster crisis, and the subsequent impact of the Great War.

Like that of other contemporaries (such as the Irish republicans enthused by the Orangemen's success in arming themselves), the perspective of Joseph Johnston – a liberal Ulster Protestant who believed his people could be won round to Home Rule – now seems naïve. However, his repudiation of the Ulster Unionist claim that civil war in Ulster was preferable to the modest reforms represented by Home Rule seems less so, particularly in the context of the 'Home Rule all round' that many expected (and which has since come to pass). In present-day Northern Ireland, where communal identities remain no less entrenched a century later, contemporary resonances can be discerned: the difficulties of sustaining support for political compromise; the pull of sectarian forces towards instability; and the appeal of intransigence, despite its counter-productive consequences, still appear relevant lessons from history.

These accounts offer many insights into the influences that shaped the revolutionary generation. The significance of the cultural nationalist revival is repeatedly encountered. The importance attached to history is particularly striking. The influence of books such as John Mitchel's *Jail Journal* and *Speeches from the Dock*; stories of 1798 and 1867; and memories of the Famine and Land War, is evident, as is the importance of commemoration, most notably of the 1798 centenary which contributed to a wider political revival leading to the formation of Sinn Féin. For republicans like Mossie Harnett and Seán Connolly, the emotional power of the story of Ireland was reinforced by its links with family and local tradition. Much of the success of the Easter rebels resulted from their appropriation of this insurrectionary tradition, and their ability to present it as a viable strategy rather than a vestige of the romantic past.

Marketed as a modern-day *Jail Journal*, Darrell Figgis's memoir of imprisonment also illustrates the republican claim to continuity. As was the case with mid-nineteenth-century Fenianism, propaganda and self-sacrifice were at least as important as revolutionary deeds in cultivating popular support. The first evidence of the republican movement's growing popularity was the success of the campaigns, largely run by women, in support of the 1916 prisoners. The executions of the Rising's leaders, and the subsequent death of imprisoned martyrs such as Thomas Ashe and Terence MacSwiney, reinforced the idea of Britain as draconian and vindictive, and of the insurrectionary tradition as a timeless struggle against tyranny.

The 'cementing of brotherhood' in Frongoch and British jails shaped the emergence of a coherent republican movement. Imprisonment could, as for Michael Collins, enhance one's political prospects or – as with Figgis and Eoin MacNeill – salvage a career blemished by failure to turn out in 1916. Conflicts within the prisons, and the wider support they generated, demonstrate the importance of nonviolent struggle after 1916. However, like other aspects of the popular mobilisation achieved by Sinn Féin – the by-elections of 1917–18, the anti-conscription campaign of April 1918, the General Election of 1918 and the establishment of Dáil Éireann in January 1919 – political activism came to be eclipsed by the armed struggle of 1919–21. Revealingly, in contrast to earlier periods when glorious failure and sacrifice were all that could be celebrated, the heroism of IRA memoirs came to overshadow the tragic appeal of prison literature.

The military dimension of the War of Independence is explored closely by two books in this series. Ernie O'Malley's account of Seán Connolly's IRA activities in the midlands and west, and Mossie Harnett's memoir of his experiences as O/C of the West Limerick Brigade's 2nd Battalion, convey the experiences of regional commanders, dealing candidly with the difficult subject matter of ambushes, executions, and the challenges of sustaining support for a campaign of guerrilla warfare. Harnett's account of his service with the anti-Treaty IRA is particularly valuable given his generation's reticence on the Civil War.

Dying for freedom – as Seán Connolly, along with five of his comrades, did at Selton Hill – also entailed killing for Ireland. The price of violence forms a central theme of P. S. O'Hegarty's *The Victory of Sinn Féin* which spans the years between 1916 and 1923.

Believing that politics rather than force should have determined the course of events after the Rising, O'Hegarty attributed the 'moral collapse' of the Irish people to the rise of the cult of the gunman and the horrors of war. Despite O'Hegarty's bleak Treatyite outlook, Harnett's account, conveying his own disillusionment with politics, illuminates many of the same concerns from a different perspective. In particular, the IRA's belief that the politicians had squandered the victory achieved by the gun contributed to the tragic events that followed the War of Independence.

The Treaty debates form the focus of Padraig de Burca and John F. Boyle's *Free State or Republic?* Based on their press reports for the *Irish Independent*, their account complements the spare (and sometimes tediously detailed) transcripts of the debates which are now available on the website of the Oireachtas. Like other first-hand sources, it conveys a sense of what it felt like to be there at the time, describing the changing mood in the chamber, the demeanour of the deputies, the manner in which they delivered their speeches, and their impact; de Valera's words, 'which electrified the assembly', clearly resonated in the Dáil in a way that they do not on the page, a reminder of a charisma of sorts lost to time. The debates divided those who advocated the Treaty as a stepping stone to full independence from those who rejected, largely on moral or ideological grounds, the right of the Dáil to disestablish the Republic. Although some may have trusted Collins's assurances on the Boundary Commission, it is striking how rarely partition features. For Irish republicans, as for British politicians like Churchill, symbolic issues centring on sovereignty such as the oath of fealty, the status of the monarch, and membership of the British Empire, were paramount.

The historian Joe Lee has described the Treaty as the occasion rather than cause of the Civil War. The failure to achieve the Republic brought to a head longstanding tensions within a party which encompassed dual monarchists, pragmatic nationalists, and separatists opposed to any link with Britain. It ignited festering tensions between rival personalities, which became further entangled with issues of political principle. Although often framed as a conflict between supporters of the Republic and those who had abandoned it, the divisions that shaped the Civil War were more complex, with de Valera's proposed alternative to the Treaty repudiated by some anti-Treaty IRA leaders. The factors that determined the stance of ordinary IRA men, which included social and class divisions as well as local rivalries, were not restricted to attitudes to the Treaty.

How do these voices from history add to our understanding of the Irish revolution? Like all useful primary sources, they complicate the picture. One of the greatest impediments to understanding the past is our knowledge of what happened next. These accounts remind us how those who lived through this era acted in the expectation of different outcomes. Prior to the outbreak of the First World War, most Irish people – including republicans – anticipated a Home Rule parliament. The conflict that many feared in 1913 was not between separatists and the British authorities but between the Ulster Volunteer Force and the British army, or between Catholic nationalists and Protestant unionists in the North. Few expected a lengthy war when Redmond declared his support for Irish enlistment in the British army in September 1914.

The value of these texts does not lie solely in the factual light they shed on past events. Like all subjective sources, they are in some respects unreliable, reflecting bias, self-importance or other limitations. Most obviously, they reflect the times in which they were written; O'Hegarty's views on women, for example, have not aged well. As a result, they illuminate mentalities, as well as the memory of the revolution, a growing area of research. Mossie Harnett was one of several thousand veterans who felt compelled to record their experiences for posterity, many doing so in the 1940s and 1950s as they themselves began to pass into history. The realisation that patriots like Seán Connolly – ordinary people who achieved remarkable things – were no longer remembered outside their own townland prompted Ernie O'Malley to write his biographical account. He was also motivated by his concern, widely shared by veterans, that their sacrifices were no longer appreciated or even understood: 'Song and story that once stirred men no longer move a younger generation.' Hence, O'Malley's determination to record, not just Connolly's story, but that of hundreds of unknown soldiers in the final decades of his life, in the hope that their stories could be 'made into a patchwork quilt from memory'. This aim alone provides a compelling reason to ensure the wider availability of eye-witness accounts, particularly during a period of commemoration in which politicians and others will claim to speak on their behalf.

Greater familiarity with contemporary sources, such as the recently digitised witness statements of the Bureau of Military History, should complicate as well as inform commemoration. Although the idealism and achievements of the founding generation will rightly be honoured in 2016, the urge to celebrate independence should be tempered by an unsentimental understanding of the process by which it was achieved. P. S. O'Hegarty's belief that the violence of the revolution killed the spirit of the national movement was shared by many after the Civil War. Violence accelerated the pace of political change, resulting in a level of independence that few anticipated before 1914, but it also narrowed the space for an accommodation between Ireland's different traditions. Despite the relative success of the republican campaign, a significant moment in the global history of anti-imperialism, Irish revolutionaries did not achieve their central aims: the restoration of Gaelic, separation from England (for many, the essence of republicanism), and a united Ireland. Nor did they fully comprehend the contradictions between the last and first two of these aims. Independence, moreover, did not always live up to expectations, as the enthusiasm of the revival gave way to a conservative State. The revolution produced losers as well as winners, including minorities on both sides of the border. It is clear from the Military Service Pensions collection that many veterans endured hardship after, as well as during, the conflict. Few, though, regretted their efforts to achieve the republic of their dreams. Despite the political complexities of the period, and the limitations of their achievements, the revolutionary generation's refusal to bend the knee against more powerful forces will continue to inspire.

Fearghal McGarry is Reader in Irish History at the School of History and Anthropology at Queen's University Belfast. His most recent book is *The Abbey Rebels of Easter 1916: A Lost Revolution* (Dublin, 2015).

Mossie Harnett c. *1915*

INTRODUCTION
James H. Joy

MOSSIE HARNETT
BIOGRAPHICAL NOTE

My father-in-law, Maurice Joseph ('Mossie') Harnett was born on 22 October 1893 in the townland of Knocknadiha, Parish of Tournafulla, County Limerick. This tiny village is near Abbeyfeale in the southwest corner of Limerick, close to Kerry on the west and Cork to the south. He was the only son of a successful farmer, also named Maurice, and Johannah Mulcahy. He had a sister Mary and two stepsisters, Brigid and Julia, from his mother's first marriage. Mossie stood to inherit at least one of his father's two substantial dairy farms, over 100 acres each. His background was not typical of the young men who would fill the ranks of the Irish Volunteers, founded in Dublin on 25 November 1913. The majority were sons of small farmers and farm labourers and sons of shopkeepers and labourers in the towns.

Harnett was influenced by many of the same ideas and forces that shaped the lives of those of his generation who took up arms in the conflict. The 1798 Centenary celebrations, the Boer War in which Irishmen fought on both sides in 1899 and 1900 and the Fenian rising in 1867 were discussed approvingly in his home. His ancestor Muiris Ó h-Airtnéide lived at Killaculleen (the farm Harnett inherited) during the Great Famine of 1845–49 and was remembered as the man who, seeing the terrible plight of so many dying in agony and distress, broke in the door of the structure erected by the authorities to store the yellow meal and doled it out to the starving people. His uncle Lar Harnett was secretary of the local branch of the Land League during the Land War in Parnell's time in the 1880s. Another uncle was Patsy Maurice Harnett, of whom he was particularly fond. In his young days he was a Fenian and helped during the Land War. He was brutally attacked at a meeting in Abbeyfeale because of his defence of Parnell at the time of the Chief's decline. He could speak Irish fluently, and was a noted musician and *seanchaí*.

A few of Harnett's teachers, influenced by the Gaelic revival or Irish-Ireland movement, tried to create an awareness of a separate Irish culture in their pupils, and to view the history of Ireland as a struggle for freedom from British rule. Harnett remembered one such teacher fondly: "Jim White was eloquent on historical events and made them come alive . . . he made us feel that our country was one to be proud of and its soldiers the bravest and finest in the land." Despite the multitude of duties on his father's farms, he tried to make time for the reading of Irish history, which he loved: "As I grew into my teens I devoured any reading material I could place my hands on, the exploits of the Fenians, the Ninety-Eight Rising, Sarsfield's Days, the Flight of the Earls . . . I wept too over our sad history, the fate of our martyrs and the unending tale of blighted hopes."

Harnett joined the Irish Volunteers in November 1915, on the formation by Ernest Blythe of a company of thirty-six men in Tournafulla and was elected captain. From early 1919 he was O/C of the 2nd Battalion, West Limerick Brigade. He had met his future wife, Julia Walsh, when she was home on leave in Kerry from her nursing duties in London during the Great War. She was the sister of Maurice Walsh the novelist, whose work *Green Rushes* was the basis of the film, *The Quiet Man*. They were married on 22 December 1920, in the parish church of Ballydonohue, near Listowel, County Kerry. They saw each other infrequently for the first year of their courtship and marriage, as Mossie had to command his battalion "on the run". After the Treaty of 1921, he took the anti-Treaty side in the Civil War and was captured and imprisoned in September of 1922. He was released at the end of 1923 and returned to Tournafulla to his wife and the year-old daughter he had never seen.

After the war Harnett returned to farming but kept up his keen interest in local and county politics. When de Valera's party, Fianna Fáil, won an overall majority of seventy-seven seats in the 1933 election, Harnett won a seat on the Limerick County Council. He received more votes than any of the other candidates and was elected to the position of Vice-Chairman of the Board of Health, where he served for seven years. In 1939 he resigned from the Council and traded his farm for another in Rathcoole, near Dublin. After a few years he sold that farm and operated a newspaper and tobacconist shop in Ranelagh, in Dublin City. In 1947 he moved his family to Swords, North County Dublin, and operated a greenhouse for tomatoes there. His daughter Betty died that year at the age of twenty of tuberculosis. His youngest daughter, Bridget, left for Washington, D.C. in the Irish Diplomatic Service in 1953, and we were married there in 1961. After Bridget left, Harnett and his wife made their last move to live with their daughter Maureen in Dun Laoghaire, South County Dublin. He helped his eldest daughter, Joan, establish a bed-and-breakfast, also in Dun Laoghaire. He died there on 29 March 1977, and was buried with full military honours. In a letter to Harnett's widow Julia, on 3 April 1977, his old Irish teacher Sylvester Conway wrote, "You have lost one of Ireland's noblest patriots who devoted the spring-time of his life to see 'our fetters rent in twain'. His was no fleeting idealism, it was his life-long ambition."

VICTORY AND WOE

Harnett first began recording his military experiences in the 1940s by submitting a number of articles to the *Kerryman*. After the Second World War the Kerryman Ltd. gathered many of these articles from I.R.A. veterans in the counties of Cork, Dublin, Kerry, and Limerick, and published paperback books with identical titles except for the identifying County name,

Mossie Harnett

e.g. *Limerick's, Fighting Story 1916–21: Told by the Men Who Made It.* The Limerick book, third in the series, was published in 1947. The chapter "The I.R.A. Campaign in West Limerick" is almost entirely Harnett's work, written under the pseudonym "Volunteer". In the opinion of the present editor, the editing of his articles along the lines of heroic and unblemished patriots made his contributions almost unrecognizable. His questioning of motives, humble self-doubt and depictions of the "underside of the revolution" are completely absent. His perceptive observations are restored in *Victory and Woe*. Over the years Harnett submitted many articles on the history of his native district to the *Limerick Leader*. In the last year of his life he was pleased to see ten brief extracts from an earlier version of *Victory and Woe* appear in a series of articles entitled "The Mossie Harnett Memoirs". The text of his narrative which appears in this work is taken from my larger interpretive work, *Victory and Woe: Mossie Harnett and the West Limerick Brigade in the Irish War of Independence 1915–1923* (Ann Arbor: UMI Dissertation Services, 2001).

Harnett included in his memoir a wealth of ideas, impressions and insights regarding the historical rationale for the struggle and his own role in the conflict, as he understood it. In particular, his candid and introspective remarks shed considerable light on the motives and aspirations of the Republican guerrillas during the conflict with the British, and their doubts and frustrations in the tragic Civil War that followed. Harnett's narrative covers the major landmarks in Irish history from the period—the founding of the Volunteers, the 1916 Easter Rising, the rise of Sinn Féin and its victory in the 1918 General Election, the founding of Dáil Éireann, the Anglo-Irish conflict, the Truce and Treaty of 1921, and the Civil War that ended in 1923.

Harnett had taken an active role in the 1918 General Election and was elected unopposed as Sinn Féin representative to the Newcastle West Rural District Council in 1919. But the press of Volunteer activities caused him to resign after a short time. Like many Volunteers, he gradually became disillusioned with the political process, and this attitude grew stronger as the guerrilla war continued. This lack of respect for the political side of the war reached a climax after the Truce and Treaty of 1921, and was probably a contributing factor in the split within the Army and the resultant Civil War. This anti-democratic sentiment is observed by Harnett in some of his reflections, e.g. "The I.R.A. believed that it was the tactics they carried out that put a halt to British rule in Ireland. It made them afterwards so reliant on force and on themselves as arbiters in our country's destiny."

Harnett wrote that the anti-Treaty I.R.A.'s heart was not in the fight when it was brother against brother: "the truth is, our hearts were not in it, and this alone contributed a good deal to our military defeat". His own humane actions support this. In one action against the Free State army, he ordered his men to fire over their heads. In another incident, he saved the life of a Free State officer and then let all of his prisoners go free. His wife Julia nursed the I.R.A. and Free State wounded without distinction as his home became a "miniature hospital". When he released other prisoners, he borrowed money and civilian clothes for them.

Mossie Harnett was a product of the political, social and cultural influences operating in early twentieth-century Ireland. The 1916 Easter Rising had a profound impact on him and formed his political values for the rest of his life. With refreshing naïveté, he believed in the ideal of an Irish Ireland, a united Irish island, and an independent Republic freed from British control. His last years were saddened by the renewal of violence in the six counties of Northern Ireland. He remained optimistic to the end, and would have agreed with the expression "Nothing fails in Ireland. It is only that the victory is delayed." In an appreciation of his life, Mainchín Seoighe wrote in the *Limerick Leader* (9 April 1977): "Mossie Harnett was one of a great generation of unselfish Irishmen, with high ideals, who were prepared to risk their all for the sake of their country and their fellow Irishmen."

Dr Edward Harnett

POSTSCRIPT

Of all the documents and narratives collected by Harnett from his fellow participants in the War of Independence, one deserves special attention. "A Hostage Looks Back" by Dr. Edward Harnett, Mossie's first cousin and predecessor as battalion commandant, describes a short-lived but particularly brutal practice instituted by the British in the spring of 1921. This is included as an appendix to this book.

VICTORY AND WOE

THE WEST LIMERICK BRIGADE IN THE WAR OF INDEPENDENCE

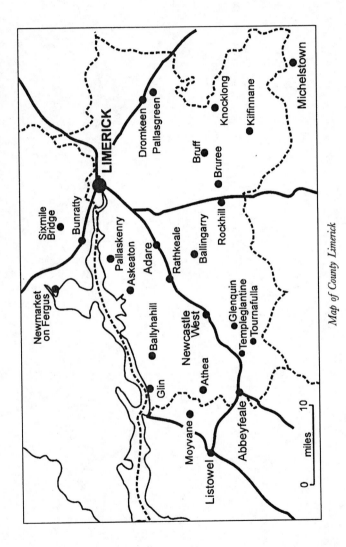

Map of County Limerick

CHAPTER I.

THE MAKING OF A REVOLUTIONARY, 1894–1914.

I was born in the townland of Knocknadiha, Parish of Tournafulla, County Limerick, towards the end of the last century. I was called Maurice Joseph Harnett and baptised in the local church. My father married into the farm where I was born and reared. My mother was a widow, had two daughters by her first husband and remained a widow for six years before marrying my father at the age of 33. He was named Maurice also, as were his immediate forebears.

Tom Murphy, my mother's first husband, was killed one dark night, when he and my mother were returning from a wedding, and the horse-drawn cart they were travelling in tumbled down a steep incline. He and my mother were pinned underneath the cart, where he died instantly. My mother escaped with slight injuries and was rescued by a passing neighbour who heard her cries for assistance.

My father brought with him a fortune of £350. He agreed to look after my step-sisters' welfare and education and gave them some money when they left the place. I must say he treated them as if they were his own daughters and they were fond of him too. On the morning following the marriage of my parents, Brigid, the elder girl, watched in wonder as my father shaved himself before a mirror on the kitchen wall. Still wondering at his actions and presence, she asked him timidly: "Are you staying long?"

At the time of the Boer War, 1899–1900, I was six years of age and can remember a little about it. I heard about the

Modder River, Tugela, Ladysmith, the defeat of General Cronje, the exploits of Botha and of the fabulous De Wet. In the years afterwards I developed a real interest in the Boer War and read all the books I could about it and its consequences for the British Empire.

Growing up had its problems and attending school was one of them. The schoolhouse I attended was only a short distance from my home and no matter how I lingered on the way, I arrived there in a quarter of an hour. Our teacher, Pat O'Donnell (a native of Killeedy) was a wiry man, of medium size and build, and ruddy complexion. He wore the usual high collar reaching to his ears, hard hat, and gaiters of yellow leather, this latter apparel to facilitate him on the horse he rode each day to the school. He lived over the mountain, about five miles distant. He was rather severe with the rod, and showed no favours.

Being barefoot at school had its hazards, I can tell you. We often stood in class, toeing a chalk line drawn in a semicircle, facing the fireplace; there the master stood as he imparted knowledge to us and questioned each nervous boy in the class. Anyone who failed to answer his question immediately got a slap of the stick on the bare shins. We were sitting ducks as the culprit jumped around on being struck, breaking up our circular formation and alarmed, he groaned and cried aloud. Our master had the devil's own time in getting us once more to toe the line. We had some real stubborn boys, nearly grown up, who resented violently undue punishment. I remember one day a boy in sixth class seized a slate in his hand and hurled it at the master's head. The master was lucky that it missed him by an inch as it smashed into smithereens on the wall behind him.

Boys, although going barefoot, always wore caps, some ragged, through which could be seen a wisp of hair sticking through. Fights were arranged during class. Any boy ready to pit his skill against another met on the road home to decide the winner, surrounded by their companions. There were some-times savage encounters, as we were nearly all semi-savage in the delight we got from witnessing these fights; a broken tooth or a black eye caused us little concern. It was a code of honour, strictly observed, that a boy who placed his right forefinger on another's forefinger and dared him to knock it off was regarded as ready to fist-fight. Otherwise he could not live down his cowardice. He was a butt for verbal and physical attacks from his schoolmates. I myself got into a situation like this once, amongst my class companions. One boy, around my age, boasted of what he would do to me and incited me to accept his challenge. So on our road home the usual ritual was observed; surrounded by our companions, we squared up to each other in a real boxing stance. Unfortunately for me, before I could steady myself, he landed on my mouth a real left, a sweeping blow which shook my teeth and brought the blood streaming from my lips. It was over in a short time, my first introduction to the manly art. Such encounters were frequent and we bore no rancour, win or lose.

We sometimes played hurling and football in an adjoining field owned by a farmer, John Kelly. We had to keep an eye on him as he did not take kindly to our presence on his land. Our hurleys were made by ourselves – sticks with a boss or turn at the end – to strike the ball with. Our slithor was usually several corks kept together by strong twine, covered with an old cloth stitched together with a shoemaker's needle. Our football was somewhat like the slithor but larger and made entirely of rags. It was a big day for me when I got a real football, a present from a kind uncle living in Dublin. Each evening, as long as it lasted, we played the game in a small field in front of our house. We were able to replace the rubber ball, inflated inside the leather cover, when worn, by an inflated pig's bladder got after the slaughter of one of these animals.

Irish history as taught then was a narrow, strict, confined subject, barely outlining events and leaving it at that. I remember Jim White as the only teacher to elaborate on the history lessons and make them come alive in a most interesting way. Some of the happiest times I spent at school were during his teaching days there; he made us feel that our country was one to be proud of and its soldiers the bravest and finest in the land. As I grew into my teens I devoured any reading material I could place my hands on: the exploits of the Fenians, the Ninety-Eight Rising, Sarsfield's days, the Flight of the Earls, and all material, truth or fiction, I eagerly read. I wept too over our sad history, the fate of our martyrs and the unending tale of blighted hopes.

Each evening after school the boys travelling along my road kept apart from the girls, whom we usually ignored even though we were not in any hurry to get home. On Friday evenings we felt that Monday morning was ages away and resentment at our treatment by the master was given vocal expression – at a safe distance from him. Some boys from the Templeglantine road called him rude names, remarked on his bow legs and on other faults that they saw in his physical build or appearance. These boys were a class apart and closely knit in fighting opponents and jealous of their townland, Templeglantine. Monday morning arrived and so too the old road boys, as usual at school. The master did not forget the rude insults of Friday evening. He held an inquisition and interrogated each of the boys involved. Holding the ash plant in a firm grip he took each boy involved in turn and gave some severe slaps on the bare hands and backsides to induce by severe punishment and pain an admission by some boy of the identity of the guilty party. One poor boy was not able to withstand the punishment, namely Paddy Keating; he revealed the names of the culprits who got their due reward by being severely slapped. Poor Paddy was then regarded as an outcast from the old road clan and had to take to short cuts by the fields to reach home safely.

Our Parish Priest Father John Reeves and curate Father Fitz paid regular visits to the school at the approach of the Bishop on his triennial visits to the parish to examine pupils being got ready for Confirmation. They were very strict in their examination of those in the confirmation class. All were expected to have a good knowledge of Christian Faith and Doctrine and of the Catechism. I was in this class one day being examined by Father John Reeves and amongst our number was a boy named John Quirke, a big burly individual.

On being asked by Father Reeves to say the corporal works of mercy, he at once in a hurry started off in fine style until the last line "Bury the dead" which he gave in a sing-song voice – "Bury the living and the dead". Father Reeves looked at him scornfully and said "Quirke, you are a bostoon, do you understand that?" Then taking him by the arm he gave him a half dozen cuts on the bare shins with a riding crop which he usually carried.

My old home in Knocknadiha where I was born and reared up to the age of fifteen years was a farm situated on the northern slope of a high hill, nearly eight hundred feet high. As a result it was a cold place in winter. It comprised one hundred and fifteen acres. It had on the high ground some arable land, some bog, and about twenty acres of heather. Lower down in the valley were a few acres of high bog, the rest reclaimed land and drained, with two large meadows of fourteen acres or so to provide hay. In this valley were extensive root and other remains of ancient forests. These provided fuel, gate posts of bog oak, and scollops of bog deal for thatching. The boundary of the farm at its lowest level was the River Allaghaun. When my father came into possession of this farm it was in a very neglected state, with bad fences, poor outhouses, and badly drained land.

He did trojan work, making drains and fences, liming and manuring the place, all of which he did in his forty years there. He was the first to build a near approach to a modern cowshed, and he erected the first hay barn in the parish, aided by a grant from the Board of Works. He was a rather stern man, though just; frivolous things he abhorred; he was kind to animals, and never would apply a whip or ashplant to horse or donkey. He built up a good herd of Shorthorn cows, and kept one of the best bulls in the parish.

This latter animal was given out to all the small farmers living near him, for service of their cows; and they were expected to give him a few days work in return—at haymaking, cutting the corn, potato digging and, especially, bringing home the harvest. Life at home at that time alternated between some study of home lessons, running messages for my mother to the local shop, and minding the cows as they grazed on the after-grass and preventing them from straying into the potato and oat crops grown in the same field. This was a job I did not like as it required vigilance to prevent the cattle from having a taste of the oats and one had to be on constant alert which did not allow any relaxation. The cows seemed to know in some uncanny way if one did not patrol along the forbidden invisible line dividing grass from crops and quickly took advantage.

Another little job I had to do was feed the cabbage into a machine which chopped it up small for pigs, poultry and cattle. Sometimes too, I had to stand beside newly-calved cows in their stalls during springtime as they were fed cooked yellow meal porridge in pecks and so prevent cows beside them from appropriating the food themselves. On many a farm then the dreaded white scour decimated the newly-born calves. This scourge left my father with only about six healthy calves out of twenty, this being the number of cows he kept. All kinds of preventative measures were taken but of no avail. My father often said that through the years he buried a fortune on the land through the loss incurred by white scour.

In the first decade of this century my father purchased a second farm, that of his deceased brother, known as Lar Maurice. The farm was situated in the townland of Killaculleen. My Aunt Mary, unmarried, lived there until her death in the mid-twenties. My father received some of the purchase price of this farm (approx. 95 acres) from my aunt out of consi-deration for being kept there until she passed away. By the time the farm was purchased I had left school, and came to reside with my aunt on this second farm. At one time we had seventeen colts, and they were the torment of my young life. No fences could contain them, and, led by a strong yellow-coloured cob, they galloped from one end of the farm to the other.

On the farm on our left, facing south, lived another uncle, known as Patsy Maurice, usually called "ould grace" from his constant prayers. He was a fine looking man, tall, ruddy complexion, blue twinkling eyes, drooped nose and placid manner. In his young days he was a Fenian, and later helped during the Land War. He was brutally attacked at a meeting in Abbeyfeale because of his defence of Parnell at the time of the Chief's decline. He could speak Irish fluently and was a noted musician and *seanchaí*.

I visited his house at night to hear him relate stories about the fairies, and tales of his youth going back to the Famine, and, of course, to listen to his music. He played the bagpipe and flute, and to his home came pipers and fiddlers from all over the South. During the First World War, though then in his old age, he developed T.B., which caused his death. In his dying bed he used to say jokingly: "*M'anam chun Diabhail*, when I pass away, put my coffin on the river nearby, and let it carry me to the sea."

Times of special note in my young life were Christmas and St. Stephen's Day. The advent of Christmas was eagerly looked forward to, and the excitement amongst my sisters and myself mounted as the day approached. My mother and father visited the shop where they bought our provisions during the year "to bring home the Christmas", as they say in rural Ireland.

It was a truly marvellous treat for myself and my sisters to be taken to this shop with them. The little presents we received from the kind shopkeeper were like manna from heaven. We never had a turkey for our Christmas dinner. Usually it was a roast goose, and a leg of ham or mutton. On Christmas Eve our excitement was at fever pitch, and as night fell so did our spirits rise, as we witnessed the departure of our servant boy and girl to rejoin their own families. The boy was regaled with porter, with a little wine for the maid.

The lighting of the Christmas candles was witnessed by us as a wonderful event. We watched as each candle was placed in a hole scooped in a sod of turf, decorated with some holly and tinsel to give the proper festive look. The candles were then placed on the sill of an uncurtained window, facing the public road, as a symbol of welcome to any homeless folk abroad that night. We all then knelt and recited the Rosary in the dimness of the kitchen, poorly lighted by a paraffin lamp hanging on the wall beside the fireplace, supplemented by the extra light of the candles.

Sitting around the fire in eager anticipation, we awaited our first taste of currant bread since the previous Christmas. As children we didn't get tea from my mother until we were about 12 years of age, but on this night the rule was broken. So imagine our joy as we drank tea from huge mugs placed on the bare deal table. We never used a tablecloth for our meals, whether on festive occasions or at any time, except when the table was got ready for the Parish Priest after he had said Mass in our kitchen, usually once a year.

My father, who usually did not take intoxicating drink to excess, on this night made some punch in a large bowl. This drink was universally prepared in all houses then, and owing to its generous proportions gave pleasure in sipping it for some hours. My father, a rather stern man, thawed out after a few drinks, was inclined to smile and chat with the family in a more sociable manner than was usual. But I can assure you I never lost my fear of him either in sober or merry mood; though I respected him I never experienced any love for him, as I received none in any manifest form from him.

Some of our neighbours spent some hours in the afternoon seeking the elusive little wren (wran) to adorn the holly bush on the following day (St. Stephen's Day) as they went in batches around the countryside from house to house collecting money, later to be used to defray the expenses of the wren dance. Jealousy arose between the various townlands as each had their own bunch of boys out that day carrying the "wran". Our neighbouring boys from Knocknadiha townland were of special interest to us, being regarded as our own. Ned Leahy, dressed in a red jacket (purloined from his mother), with white-striped trousers, and high hat festooned with streamers of various hues was an example of the mode of dress worn. Ned was a musician of note on the fiddle; the bodhran was tapped in rhythm by Sonny Brown. There were a number of dancers and a good singer to sing the wrenboys song:

> The wren, the wren, the king of all birds,
> St. Stephen's Day he was caught in the furze,
> Although he was little, his family was great,
> So cheer up landlady and give us a treat.

So it continued with many more lines to make for great merriment and enjoyment.

Wrenboys, hungry from traipsing around the countryside from early morning, appreciated the gifts of currant bread often given to them. They were not all backward in slipping a cake under the folds of their jackets, if the occasion arose. A cake of this soda bread of generous proportions and equally generous supply of currants and raisins in its composition was consumed between them with relish.

No wrenboys left any farmhouse kitchen without playing some jigs or reels for their best dancer who took his stand on the big flagstone in front of the fireplace where he executed the intricacies of the dance, to the delight of the members of the household. Money was scarce in my youth and a couple of shillings given to a batch of wrenboys was regarded as a generous gift. In our house money was really scarce, and my father did not take too kindly to this custom. He doled out his few shillings amongst his favourite wrenboys sparingly. Strange wrenboys from outside the parish often went away empty-handed after a good deal of argument. Their reluctance to leave such inhospitable reception often caused me, as a youngster, some heart pangs. To me the wrenboys with their strange dress and generally frightening apparel, as rushing into our yard they played on the bodhrans, created a thrill of pleasurable awe and fear in my breast.

In my youth, Christmas without St. Stephen's Day and the wrenboys was almost meaningless. All day I watched for their arrival—living on a sloping hillside I could espy them afar off, and note their progress. Our few public houses did a good business too, as carrying the "wran" was thirsty work, each batch of grown up young boys did justice to each pint of porter served out, some gratis too. These pints added to the enjoyment of the day, and as evening approached many a wrenboy was in a maudlin, hilarious mood.

In my youth primitive conditions prevailed in the rural community with the bare minimum of comfort in the homes of the people. Owing to the scarcity of farm buildings, due to shortage of money, as prices were at starvation level for farm produce, as well as a tyrannical landlord system, it was customary to rear farm animals in their infancy in the kitchen of the farmhouse. This was the cause of great discomfort to all its occupants, as the smell that permeated the kitchen from these animals was disgusting in the extreme. It is hard now to envisage, in our modern environment, all the discomforts endured by our rural community fifty years ago. The family had to sit at the kitchen table in the same rude surroundings, eat their meals and inhale the unsavoury perfume emanating from these animals in the confines of a farm kitchen. Our primitive state and ignorance robbed us of the elemental joys of life.

In our daily lives, brutality was never too far absent and the veneer of civilisation in our actions was quickly forgotten and ever ready to be submerged as occasion warranted. Violence was common as an arbitration for disputes with many, side by side with genuine kindness and hospitality. Being as we were, conditioned physically and mentally by our environment, it was no wonder that our actions sometimes were harsh and cruel. Every Sunday in our little village, after consuming an excess of intoxicating liquor, fights were common between neighbours and blood was spilt to disgrace the Lord's Day. Some defiant spirits, even in defeat, at a safe distance hurled epithets and invective abuse to try to recompense themselves for their often hasty retreat.

In my father's house in my childhood and early youth, a welcome awaited the very poor traveller of the roads. These people differed from what we now call itinerants, and they usually begged singly and not in groups. They were to be seen

on every road in South Munster, but were in their greatest
numbers in Cork, Kerry, and West Limerick. They mostly
came from towns and villages, and were almost at starvation
level, their sad plight frequently having been brought about by
the loss of their families through emigration or death. They
often got shelter at night in farmers' kitchens, where they were
provided with beds of straw or hay beside the wall, and where
they benefited from the heat of a large turf fire. I can remember
seeing in our own warm kitchen my father arranging their
sleeping quarters when the rest of the household had retired
for the night. We only kept men travellers, and never more
than two at a time. Their inadequate bedclothes depended on
the clothes or rags they wore, as little could be provided by the
women of the house, because of short supply.

Keeping these travellers caused a great deal of inconven-
ience and annoyance to the household in general. It upset the
usual routine; and the morning chores, such as cooking,
cleaning, etc., were disrupted by the presence of such untidy
people around the place. But people were not as fastidious
then as nowadays, and in their charity they put up with such
upsets, grumbling and scolding as they sometimes did, but
accepting the hardships as part of their duty towards their
fellow men.

On summer evenings, when the day's toil was over,
young boys and girls met at the crossroads, the boys usually
sitting on the fence, or else engaged in playing hurling or
football in some nearby field, or engaging in contests in
jumping, running, weight-throwing, lifting, or tug-of-war. The
young girls paraded along the road, arm in arm, laughing and
chatting, and exchanging pleasantries with the boys. It was all
very pleasant then, in the springtime of life at its best, but this
carefree world would vanish in the trials of the years ahead.
Young girls were in the majority in possessing level heads, and
though maybe some were romantic, the most of them were
nearly always ready to subordinate love and its lure in favour
of securing a good home, a hard-working husband and a
secure future.

Good dancers were in abundance, and it was a pleasure to attend a crossroad dance, and see the wonderful performance of graceful girls and boys as, with nimble feet, they went through the set dances, polkas, barn dances, eight-hand reels. The fiddle player was rewarded at the end of the dance when the hat was passed round. The amount put into the hat by each person was usually a penny, and the total takings were rarely more than 2*s.* 6*d.*—about the daily wage of a farm labourer at the time. Our parish clergy cast a cold eye on the crossroad dances, regarding them as places of promiscuous lovemaking!

It was a time and atmosphere in which one relaxed effortlessly in such genial company without any worries for the morrow, as at that time in Ireland there was no regimentation of anyone. Time was practically limitless, stretching to a pattern of life in frugal comfort. There was contentment with one's lot, and generally a happy family, so what more could one want? In the majority of cases, "except for the restless ones who ventured over the hill", all the others preferred to live and die amongst the neighbours they knew from childhood, and whose way of life they were familiar with.

CHAPTER II.

A TERRIBLE BEAUTY IS BORN, 1915-1918.

Prior to the Great War (1914-18), our political outlook was governed by John Redmond and the Irish Party. The majority of the people gave him their support. We had a minority in our parish, however, who gave their allegiance to William O'Brien's "All for Ireland" Party.

Conditioned by the conversations of my immediate relatives, I supported John Redmond, Parnell's successor. Home Rule for Ireland by constitutional methods would then have satisfied most of us. But times were to change, as young men with new gospels brought us a new awareness of Irish nationhood. The outbreak of the Great War in 1914 turned the thoughts of these young men to making a fight for the freedom of their own land. And so was born the Irish Volunteer movement. I was caught up in these stirring events, and on the formation of a company of the Irish Volunteers in our parish of Tournafulla in November 1915 I joined up. The company was organised by Ernest Blythe, a Northern Presbyterian, and a fluent Irish speaker. He raised companies in about ten parishes—about 300 men—and officers were duly appointed for each company.

The whole made up a small battalion, the overall commander of which was Charlie Wall of Dromcollogher. Our equipment was poor, consisting of some dozen Mauser rifles, some revolvers, about a dozen shotguns per company, and some '98 style pikes. At the inauguration of the Tournafulla Company I was elected captain, Tommy Leahy was elected 1st lieutenant and Tom Sullivan 2nd lieutenant. The total strength of the company was thirty-six men and boys. We met each week for drill formation. I was, of course, a novice at the business. A British Army Manual (procured somehow) provided all the necessary instructions for the instructor. I picked up, too, a book on guerrilla warfare, which explained and elaborated on the use of hedges, banks and cover, useful in ambush, by small bodies of men. We also learned semaphore signalling, a special section reaching a high degree of proficiency at it.

The people in general looked on us as madmen. They thought that with our poor equipment it would be childish to engage the British Army and armed police. The big farmers did not give us much support, our best friends being among the small farmers and labourers. Well-to-do shopkeepers in the towns derided our efforts and were hostile to us.

From the commencement of the year 1916 I and the officers of our company kept up intensive training with our men on one night each week, and also on Sundays after Mass. We carried out exercises all over the fields in the locality. I often marched our men several miles over rough roads to take part in mock skirmishes with the whole battalion. Though we were all engaged during the week at farm work, no one ever failed to turn up on these occasions. I myself, in the springtime had to fodder about forty young cattle, clean out the shed, rush to Mass, eat a quick dinner and later march long distances to the field where we manoeuvred, then return on foot at night and again fork in hay to feed hungry animals.

On St. Patrick's Day, 1916, the whole battalion marched to Newcastle West to take part in a parade in the Square. From Tournafulla to Newcastle West was a distance of eight miles. Our company was led by myself and Lieutenants Leahy and Sullivan, with our local fife and drum band out in front. On entering the Square we were assailed by soldiers' wives and friends, who hurled verbal abuse at us, as well as rotten eggs and other missiles. But we ignored them and kept our lines intact. The wives and families of men serving overseas were very hostile to the Volunteers.

The platform—a long car owned by Dinny MacAuliffe—was in the centre of the Square. It was draped in green and gold, and over it flew a Tricolour. On the platform stood Fr. Michael Hayes, CC, Fr. Tom Wall, CC, Ernest Blythe, and the guest speaker, Seán MacDermott. Our enthusiasm was unbounded, our cheers deafening as we applauded each speaker. Here in this town history was being unfolded and as we listened to Seán MacDermott's passionate, emotional, yet reasoned speech, his words imprinted his spirit and courage in our hearts.

When the meeting was over each volunteer, on being disbanded, made for the nearest public house where each, according to his taste, drank porter, whiskey or lemonade, bought some baker's bread to eat, washed down by a drink. This was our diet to sustain us after our long march, and long time spent standing in ordered ranks listening to the speakers. We were a hardy breed and could endure a lot of hardship in those days.

Time marched on, and our company kept up its training in preparation for the day when a blow would be struck for our country's freedom. When Easter Sunday, 1916, arrived, we, ordinary Volunteers, were not aware of its significance. I was notified on Easter Saturday to mobilise our company next day, and to march with all the available arms to a mobilisation of the battalion at Glenquin Castle, three miles away. This I did, and arrived at the Castle early in the day. At Glenquin Commandant Charlie Wall, assisted by Major Jimmy MacInerney, director of operations, from Limerick city, reviewed the Volunteers. Also present were the patriotic priests, Fr. Tom Wall and Fr. Michael Hayes.

On the green lawn in front of the castle we dressed our ranks. Looking on was a large party of armed R.I.C. in formation on the road. Some of our men had rifles or shotguns; but most had no firearms. A few carried '98 style pikes. I can still remember Major MacInerney's green uniform, its gold shamrock embroidery and epaulettes, and the large Webley revolver and gleaming sword he wore. Another memory is of

Volunteer Tadhg Collins, Monagae Company, carrying a long pike. Tadhg was a remarkable character, tall and bony, with a pale complexion, intelligent face, blue eyes, and a long pointed nose. He had just returned from the Irish Ecclesiastical College in Paris. He had been studying there for the priesthood, but left for some reason—probably he hadn't a vocation. He was outspoken in his views, and did not believe in conforming either to church or state. His dedication to the cause of freedom was genuine and selfless.

After some hours of manoeuvres we were dismissed, still in the dark about the historic events taking place in Kerry, or the reason for our mobilisation, or the countermanding order that had decided that we were not to take the field that day. But even the dullest of us knew that something of importance had occurred, or was about to take place. All the evidence pointed to that. There was the presence of the priests, and the high-ranking officer from Limerick. We had noticed too the bread van, labelled 'Brodericks Bread, Broadford', filled with bread, which was drawn up on the road. The bread was to have been distributed to the men who were to have risen in arms that day. So ended our futile endeavour. And as we marched homewards the heavens opened, and the rain fell in torrents.

Easter Monday was a bright, warm day, as is usual in late spring. That afternoon I tackled the ass to the cart to take some dozens of eggs to sell at Leahy's shop in Tournafulla. This was something I usually did for my aunt. I bought groceries for the house at Leahy's, bartered for by the eggs. As I slowly wended my way homewards I was accosted by an R.I.C. man named Bourke who, in a short chat, informed me of the Rising in Dublin, and of the sinking of the arms ship, the Aud, and of the capture of Casement on Good Friday. I was dismayed at the news, and hurried home, impatient to tell everyone what I had just heard.

Next morning I cycled into Newcastle West where I met some Volunteers, and we discussed the possibility of trying to reach Dublin. Dan Ronan of the Monagae Company was emphatic in his views, and was determined to get to Dublin. However, after a lengthy discussion, we agreed there was nothing we could do as individuals without specific orders from our Commandant. Garbled news continued to reach us about events in Dublin. At the end of the week the truth finally reached us.

Nearly everybody was astounded by the news; people generally were bewildered, and comments were not favourable. This was understandable, as most of the country was still behind John Redmond's policy. The subsequent executions and deportations were soon to change the people's attitude radically, and reverse the pacifist acceptance of the constitutional movement. West Limerick men deported were Charlie Wall, Garrett McAuliffe, Matt Flanagan, J. Dore, Paddy Sheehan, Con Collins and Patrick Mulcahy of Monagae, who fought with the Citizen Army. But it was the execution of Con Colbert, and the drowning of Donal Sheehan of Monagae on his way to meet Casement, that affected us most of all, and that determined us to vindicate them and emulate their sacrifice on freedom's altar if necessary.

Things remained quiet during the remainder of the year 1916. I and my comrades of the Volunteers no longer drilled as before but maintained contact with each other. The people were coming round to the idea that at least things would never be the same again. It was at this time too that innumerable badges with pictures of the executed leaders found favour and ready sale. Green-white-and-orange flags were displayed, both large and small, hurling and football teams turned out to play in the national colours. People wore ganseys, ties, ribbons and socks in the Republican colours. Danny Rahilly of Rockchapel went so far as to paint his milk cans in the colours.

On Easter Saturday night, 1917, Jim Colbert, Bill Carroll, Mick Roche and Con Mullane, all of Athea, spent until 2 a.m. hoisting national flags on the topmost branches of trees in, and on trees bordering the roads leading into Athea village, where Con Colbert had spent his youth. Having tied the flags securely on the tree tops, Con Mullane cut off all the branches as he descended, thus making it impossible for anyone to climb the trees and remove the flags.

In Tournafulla, a green-white-and-orange flag was placed on the chimney of the tallest house in the village by Jack Aherne (known as The Private). All the ladders in the area were hidden after the erection of the flag, so that the police could not remove it. It stayed aloft for a considerable time, flowing proudly and defiantly in the breeze.

Things rested so until the summer of 1917 when we heard the news of the internees' release from English prisons. This caused great excitement and jubilation. Two important prisoners of note from West Limerick were amongst those released. They were Dr. Richard Hayes, who fought with the North County Dublin Volunteers during Easter Week, and Con Collins, an associate of Austin Stack in the attempt to land arms at Tralee.

Tommy Leahy and myself organised and led a large enthusiastic party, headed by our band with flags waving to Rathkeale where thousands of people were assembled to welcome them home. It was an occasion to remember; the excitement and cheering was tremendous. All nature was in harmony with the event, the sun shone down in splendour, the fields were in glory with summer flowers and the hedges and trees clothed with abundant green foliage. It looked a good augury for a nation struggling to freedom.

The prisoners, on their release, began the task of once again organising the Volunteers. Here in West Limerick former officers began enthusiastically to re-form companies and our organisation extended to cover all West Limerick. As this was taking place it was found necessary to establish Sinn Féin cumann and build up a political movement embracing all the people ready to subscribe to its principles. Both the Volunteers and Sinn Féin worked in collaboration.

At the end of 1917 we became keen supporters of the Gaelic revival. The schoolhouse was placed at our disposal where we attended Irish classes once a week in the evenings. About thirty boys and girls attended, of various ages from 16 to 30 years. Our teacher was Sylvester Conway, a native of Tipperary. He had a tough, hard time in bad weather, cycling to all the parishes in a radius of eight miles from Abbeyfeale.

On St. Patrick's Day, 1918, I and a few of the boys held a collection for the Gaelic League outside the church gate at Tournafulla. We collected £15, a very large sum for that time. I received a special letter of thanks for our effort from the general secretary of the Gaelic League.

Prior to the 1917 Clare By-Election, Tommy Leahy and myself held a church gate collection in aid of the election fund. It took some courage to ask for money. The big farmers cast a cold eye on our table as they passed in to Mass. One man paused as he was passing by, and Tommy Leahy asked him for support for the Sinn Féin candidate, Eamon de Valera, as against Paddy Lynch, Crown Prosecutor for Clare. He looked at us with scorn as he emphatically said: "I'll support the Crown Prosecutor."

Our first Brigade Commandant of the reorganised Volunteers in 1917 was Tom O'Shaughnessy, but he resigned after a short period. The man elected Brigade O/C to replace him was Sean Finn, a native of Rathkeale. Sean was a lovable character, young, handsome, athletic, a universal favourite. I got to know him first at a Volunteer Convention held in Croke Park in November, 1917, which was presided over by Michael Collins.

Our local Battalion, comprising five companies, had Dr. Edward Harnett as its O/C during 1917 and part of 1918. He, too, resigned but remained in the Volunteers as medical officer to the Second Battalion. Our Brigade comprised five Battalions, the total approximate strength of the Brigade being about twelve hundred men. Each Battalion had as centre the nearest local town, these being Newcastle West, Abbeyfeale, Rathkeale, Dromcollogher and Glin-Ballyhahill.

Madame Markievicz addressed a large meeting in Athea, the home town of Con Colbert, shortly after her release from prison in 1917. Whilst all these exciting events were taking place the people had still to see after their daily affairs, buying and selling and attending to the never-ending tasks that call to be done from the cradle to the grave.

The farmers' and labourers' lot improved noticeably from 1917 onwards. Prices for cattle rose steeply—around £60 for in-calf heifers, £20 to £30 for stores, £30 for fat sow pigs, with corresponding high prices for bacon pigs, milk, sheep, poultry, eggs and all kinds of farm produce. Agricultural labourers benefited, and their wages rose from £12 a year that was formerly paid to £40 to £45 pounds.

Agricultural feeding stuffs rose in price too, and it was customary to pay £3 for a twenty stone sack of Indian meal. Rationing of sugar and other commodities was enforced as a war measure by the British government. Pollard was mixed with the flour, giving the latter only a remote resemblance to the real thing. It was a real laxative, and nobody who ate it ever required medicine. In church at Sunday Mass a striking odour filled the place as the gases it created escaped into the atmosphere. One of the results of the good prices paid for cattle, milk, etc., was that farmers now bought pony traps to travel in more comfort than formerly. It says a good deal in their favour that the support most of them gave us in the Volunteers was now given from a position of comfort hitherto unknown to the majority of them.

During 1918 we had reorganised and retrained our Volunteer company in Tournafulla. We gave every assistance too to the Sinn Féin cumann which met at Davy Sheehan's. Davy, called "The King", was a bachelor labourer, living alone in a small thatched dwelling. He was middle-aged, a sturdy build of a man, dark complexion, and spoke rather rapidly, and was cranky. He was a staunch supporter of the Volunteers, Sinn Féin and the G.A.A. He talked about some farmers' nice daughters living nearby and thought his chances as a good looking bachelor were not too remote . . . alas, his hopes never came to fruition!

During all this time I was very busy with work on the farm, as well as attending parades, political meetings, assemblies, dances and Battalion Councils. My time was completely occupied. I paid many visits to Newcastle West to attend meetings of the Comhairle Ceanntair Sinn Féin for West Limerick. One of our most successful dances was held in the local school in 1918. Our curate, Fr. Michael Twomey, attended, and sang several patriotic songs. Father Michael Hayes, Newcastle West, also attended, and delivered a marvellously stirring oration to the assembled young men and women. Our guest singers were from Abbeyfeale, Dromcollogher and Newcastle West. They were splendid singers.

I was usually appointed Master of Ceremonies at these gatherings in my own parish. Many's the nice girl I flirted with at these dances, and in neighbouring parishes as well. *Feisheanna*, sports and dances occupied our time almost every Sunday. The young girls at that time were filled with patriotic ardour, and showed this by their preference for the men and officers of the Volunteers.

As I was living with my aunt at this time, I was free of parental control. My parents did not take too kindly to the new movement, now sweeping the country; and in no uncertain terms I was informed of their views and of their disapproval of the course I was following. My aunt led a lonely life, and being a person with political views inherited from her association with the constitutional movements of Parnell, and then Redmond, was reluctant to accept or approve of this business of armed resistance. I lived with her from 1916 to 1920.

It was only during periods of turf cutting, hay making and harvesting that we had any company. I being young, this lonely life my aunt led did not bring any realisation to me of the great sadness she must so often have felt as she contemplated her long past happy girlhood and young womanhood. For her the present meant little as she sat all day near the turf fire, in complete isolation. Her only occupation was the cooking of our simple meals, and caring for some hens, chickens and geese she kept.

My life at that time, as I've said, was a very full one, and with the thoughtlessness of youth, I'm afraid that my actions showed little concern, thought or sympathy for her lonely life.

I was totally engrossed in national affairs, and in selfish interests of my own, and I did not give her the sympathy I now know I should have given her. The difference in sex, age and outlook didn't help to make communication easy.

Many a lonely night she sat near the fire awaiting my return from some dance, political meeting, or military exercise, as she recited the Rosary to herself in that isolated house. Hearing my footsteps on my return, she usually unlocked the kitchen door, standing inside it just as she opened it for me. On one occasion, hearing my footsteps approach, as she thought, she lifted the latch off the door, and opened it, only to discover nobody there. She was terrified, and nearly collapsed. She informed me of this, when, to her great relief, I arrived a short time later. She never complained to me or my father about my late nights out. The incident of the footsteps coming to the door, and later happenings in our house, caused her to have a severe nervous breakdown from which she never recovered.

During 1918 it was evident that John Redmond's Party, with its policy of co-operation in England's war efforts, was losing support. They won a few by-elections in the North and one in Waterford where the Redmonite following was strong. The Volunteers gave support by their discipline and numbers in protecting Sinn Féin meetings against the rough tactics employed by their opponents. This year saw a drying up of recruits for the British Army. No longer did the drums, the music or the glamour of khaki-clad armed soldiers parading the towns evoke the response of formerly; this one-time flood was reduced to a trickle and this continuing trend alarmed the Army and British government.

The threat of conscription in 1918 by Lloyd George, the British Prime Minster, gave a great impetus to the Volunteer movement. It brought hundreds of young men to swell the ranks of Volunteers but only for a short period, for as soon as that menace was over our ranks were again depleted. The pledge to resist conscription got the approval of the Irish Hierarchy. Their Pastoral Manifesto was read out at all Masses throughout the country by the clergy. This Pastoral approved of all means consonant with the law of God. Our Parish Priest, Rev. J. Reeves, after reading the Manifesto took somewhat from its intended meaning by a short address to the congregation afterwards. I and the officers of the local Volunteers and Sinn Féin cumann took exception to the remarks he made. At a meeting afterwards of the Sinn Féin cumann a unanimous resolution was passed censuring his statement. It was agreed that a statement of our views disagreeing with him be brought to the Parochial House by a deputation of half-a-dozen members representing both organisations. I was selected to read this statement, assisted by Danny Curtin, our adjutant, as an active vocal supporter. It was my first clash with the clergy in an interpretation of our views on national affairs. He did not like what he heard and said so in no uncertain manner. Danny and I were not forgiven until he was transferred elsewhere. He then sent for our respective fathers before leaving and informed them that we were forgiven for our conduct.

After this clash, until he left in 1919, I dared not approach him for the use of the school or to notify him for his approval of the invitations our cumann sent to priests in other parishes to speak at functions we organised. This I had to leave to Tommy Leahy, our 1st lieutenant, to secure his permission for all such speakers.

One oireachtas that we held during 1918 remains in my memory vividly still. We held this function in a field near the church on a sunny Sunday afternoon in. Hundreds of people, young and old, attended to enjoy the singing, the dancing and listening to the speakers, who were Con Collins, one of the released prisoners, Father Tom Wall, and Father Michael Hayes. At all these places of entertainment we usually held collections, which were very necessary to keep our movement provided with money. Tommy Leahy and another boy collected this cash at the gateway. As they stood there two policemen approached them, Constables Lyons and Bourke. Tommy said that they would have to pay to enter like all the rest. They objected and used strong language as they tried to force their way in. Tommy physically tried to stop them but without success. During the address by Father Wall they heard many nasty stories about themselves and the police force they were members of. The police left when all was over and their manner and demeanour boded no good for someone.

The following evening they demonstrated their hostility to their opponent, Tom Leahy. Tom, on the following afternoon, rode an old farm horse to the creamery for some butter for his mother. On his way he had to pass the R.I.C. barracks and was observed as he did so. Coming home by the same route Constable Lyons met him, seized the reins of the horse and tried to unseat him. Tom instinctively lifted his leg and gave Lyons a kick in the chest and in the encounter lost his parcel of butter. He rode down the road a short distance, tied his horse to a furze bush, came back, and courageously retrieved his butter. That night, 6 September 1918, was a dark foggy one and under the shelter of some overhanging bushes by the roadside near the village two policemen waited in ambush. Their purpose was to beat up Tom Leahy for they knew he visited the village nearly every night on some business or other. They were right. On this very night his uncle Jer. Mulcahy had requested him to buy a bottle of whiskey and bring it home to him. He did so and sauntered down the road on his way home with the bottle held in his hand. As he was passing by where the two policemen lay hidden, they jumped out to attack him. He instinctively turned and ran back the way he had come, drawing from his coat pocket a loaded revolver he possessed. He ran about thirty yards, with the police close at his heels, and just as Lyons tried to grapple with him Tommy turned and in so doing fell with Lyons on top of him. As he fell Tom pulled the trigger and shot Lyons through the thigh. He groaned as the bullet hit him. Immediately Bourke, the second policeman, fired his revolver at Tom, but missed him because of the darkness of the night. In the confusion Tom escaped, assisted by friendly neighbours. As a result he could not sleep at home for many a long day afterwards.

So I had in our Volunteer company my 1st lieutenant, one of the first boys in Ireland at that period to engage the police with a lethal weapon. It was but the prelude to all that followed in the months ahead.

Events at that period followed rapidly one after another. The Great War was coming to a close and ended in November. For us came the task of winning the General Election of 1918. The result was a clear mandate, given by the people to our elected representatives to implement the Proclamation of Easter Week. This they did on 21 January 1919, sitting assembled in the Mansion House in Dublin, where before the eyes of the world they unanimously declared Ireland a Republic. All this in defiance of the mightiest empire that was ever seen since creation.

CHAPTER III.

A NATION ONCE AGAIN, 1919.

21 January 1919 will be forever remembered in our land. Two important events occurred on that date: one was the Proclamation of Independence, declaring Ireland a Sovereign Republic, reaffirming our right to freedom as defined by Padraig Pearse from the steps of the G.P.O. on Easter Monday.

Dáil Éireann, meeting in the Mansion House, by the unanimous decision of our freely elected representatives, representing the majority of the Irish people, declared to the world that henceforth we'd make our own laws to administer the affairs of the country and owe no allegiance to any foreign power, and to recognise the Volunteers to be the people's army who would be known from that day forward as "The Irish Republican Army". What really electrified us all was the armed attack on the R.I.C. at Soloheadbeg on that historic day.

During the Peace Conference at Versailles, following the end of the war, a delegation from America, Messrs. Dunne, Walsh, and Ryan, arrived in Ireland. They were the selected representatives of the Irish organisations in the U.S.A. to put Ireland's case demanding recognition before the Peace Conference. As the stated aim of the Allies was the right of small nations everywhere to be free, it was their intention to place Ireland's case for such recognition to be sanctioned by them. Well, historic Limerick accorded them on their arrival an overwhelming welcome by Corporation and all public bodies. Every Volunteer company in the County and City assembled there, and lined O'Connell Street on both sides for its entire length. Clare too was not found wanting on that day and brought in a large number of Volunteers. The whole parade was under the command of Michael Brennan, Meelick, Co. Clare. Our Volunteer company numbering about thirty-six men marched to Devon Road Railway Station under my command, assisted by our two lieutenants to detrain at Limerick and take part in the reception. We wore for the first time green military caps with the badge Óglaigh na hÉireann, leather belts and haversacks. All paid their own expenses for the day. The British armed forces were deployed in strength, consisting of several lorries of troops and police. These drove up O'Connell Street perilously close to our ranks to try and create disorder. This they failed to do as Michael Brennan, in full uniform, by his cool manner and marked defiance of their might assisted by Volunteer officers kept our ranks intact.

As everyone knows, Ireland's efforts to get recognition failed, owing to the machinations of British Prime Minister Lloyd George and the weakness of the American President Wilson, who mouthed the Doctrine of Freedom for all people so that they become masters of their destiny. It was grand to apply the principle to the downtrodden in the lands of their now defeated enemies. It was outrageous that the serfs in Ireland dare demand such recognition from kind-hearted Mother England, their benefactor in famine and peril.

Early in that year I was promoted to the rank of battalion commandant, 2nd Battalion, West Limerick Brigade I.R.A. This involved the promotion of Tom Leahy to the rank of captain in our company and the appointment of William Horgan as 1st lieutenant. In lieu of guns and rifles for training purposes we now used wooden guns and sometimes hurleys. I held manoeuvres one day in the immediate vicinity of the police barracks. We surrounded the building—a two storied structure isolated in a field facing the road in front. Our proceedings must have looked real to the police, watching from inside. We advanced towards the building, in extended formation, taking advantage of the cover provided by fences surrounding it. We kept up these tactics for a considerable time and without incident withdrew as we lined up on the road in front to march away. The police then were hated and in our district Constable Lyons, now recovered from his wound, and Bourke were specially marked as two opponents to be kept in mind as our deadly enemies. I met Constable Bourke shooting game on our land and ordered him to betake himself off. He reluctantly left after some hot words had passed between us.

I was now at this period in command of five company areas, namely Abbeyfeale (not yet organised), Athea, Templeglantine, Mount Collins and Tournafulla. To complete the strength of the battalion by the inclusion of Abbeyfeale was most necessary. To do this work some boys from Abbeyfeale approached me, namely Jimmy Collins, Larry Harnett and Paddy O'Neill. This I agreed to do, assisted by Tommy Leahy and Jack Aherne. A meeting place was fixed at Jack Larry Collins's old cowshed at Mount Mahon crossroads, just a quarter of a mile from the town. The meeting took place at night, and approximately eighty young men assembled there to take the oath to serve faithfully in the I.R.A., and obey all lawful commands. The election of officers was by secret ballot; each put on a slip of paper the candidate of his choice. It looked good for the confidence placed in him that Jimmy Collins, by a great majority, was elected as company captain—being then around nineteen years of age. In that and other companies during the years following, until July 1921, many different officers had to be appointed to all these posts, as owing to arrest, imprisonment, death, and loss by the absence of those forced "on the run", this was so. It was necessary now, too, after the reorganisation of the companies that a battalion staff be appointed. This was done at a combined meeting of the officers of the five companies, presided over by myself as O/C. Jimmy Collins was the unanimous choice for the rank of vice-commandant; it spoke well for his popularity. Danny Murphy, Abbeyfeale (a grand young man) was elected as quartermaster and Jack Aherne, Tournafulla as adjutant.

During this period raids by the police in homes of prominent officers in the I.R.A. were of frequent occurrence. Early one morning in the spring of 1919 my home in Killaculleen was searched for arms by a party of police who surrounded the house at dawn. Lucky for me I got time to conceal a revolver and ammunition I possessed in a large bucket full of potatoes. Standing in view on the kitchen floor, these completely covered the revolver and ammunition. I had only just concealed these incriminating weapons as the police, with thunderous knocks, battered at the kitchen door and hall door. I reluctantly let them in as I listened to the abuse levelled at me. One of the first policemen to rush in was Bourke, who roughly pulled me about as the others rushed into the rooms, including my aunt's, in search of arms and incriminating documents.

Having found nothing they withdrew in an ugly mood— being disappointed at their fruitless search. If they had come to search on the previous night things would have probably had a different complexion and maybe dangerous outcome. On that night Tom Leahy, Jack Aherne and myself were in the house. Before retiring to bed we all exhibited our hardware for examination between us, then we tumbled into our respective beds. Tom Leahy and Jack Aherne in one and I in another in adjoining rooms. We placed our revolvers under the pillows for instant use if required. Tom Leahy was wanted by the authorities for his shooting of Constable Lyons. Jack Aherne was ever ready to act quickly on impulse; you may imagine what would have happened in such a circumstance, being surrounded or trapped with loaded weapons. On looking back now I think that we were lucky in not being confronted by such a dire responsibility.

During this period we called at several farmers' houses to commandeer the guns that they owned. Sometimes we met with resistance and violent hostility. One Sunday morning we raided a farmhouse, quite near where I lived. Our party included Tom Leahy, Jack Aherne, Peadar Clancy and myself. Peadar Clancy was a wanted man "on the run", and actually a stranger to us. We got two splendid double-barrelled shot-guns. Violent resistance came to us from an old man in his seventies. In fact it was lucky for us that the owners of the guns were at Mass. That afternoon Jack Terry O'Connor, who owned one of the guns, came to me demanding his weapon back. He threatened me with dire consequences if it was not returned. At that time the police were also collecting all the guns they could find belonging to registered owners to forestall us. They were aware of our efforts to collect same. On the day following our successful seizure of these guns a large party of police visited the same house to secure possession of these weapons. Naturally we were delighted at being successful by such a short head. Guns, revolvers and a few rifles were seized during this period all over the West Limerick Brigade area.

One Sunday afternoon, in two commandeered motor cars, Ned Cregan, Paddy Aherne, Ned Ryan, Tom Leahy and myself carried out a raid for arms in the Abbeyfeale district. We searched selected houses of persons thought to be hostile to us. On approaching the house of one of these, a large farm house, the door was slammed in our faces. Leading our party was Tom Leahy and myself and as we ran towards the closed door a shot was fired from inside, through the door. It slightly wounded me on the right hand. We all rushed close up to the protecting walls of the farm house; threatened to throw a bomb into the kitchen and open fire through the windows if the door was not opened to admit us. At the same time we shouted loudly that we were the I.R.A. collecting guns. This had the desired effect as we were admitted to collect the weapons.

Next house on our list was the home of Walter Broderick, a Lieutenant in the British Army. There we got a splendid Colt revolver and a shotgun. We met no resistance. In our raids ammunition was of utmost importance so we made sure to get some with the weapons. From there we went to the house of Maurice Wolfe at Cratloe. During the war he was a 1st Lieutenant in the Dublin Fusiliers. There we got some shotguns and cartridges after being strongly obstructed in our search. Ned Ryan took strong objection to this behaviour, and pointing his gun around, threatened to blow the brains out of anyone not staying quiet. In the confusion created we missed a fine revolver owned by Maurice, later confiscated by the

Black and Tans . They seized it from him as well as threatening to shoot him despite his statement that he was an ex-army officer.

Coming back from Cratloe, we drove into Abbeyfeale town, despite the fact that a strong force of police was stationed there. In the town we met some of the local I.R.A. boys who took us to the home of an ex-policeman, named Billy Gahan. From him we seized a shotgun and some cartridges. On hearing that we were in town, a well-known and popular lady, Miss L. Leahy, belonging to a leading patriotic family, came to me and said that Dan, her brother, wished to hand over to us a shotgun he owned. Of course we accepted it thankfully, and expressed our gratitude to his sister. In the great O'Connell's time it was at Leahys hostelry that the horses were changed and fresh ones provided to pull the mail coach on the road to Dublin. Daneen Dan, a noted leader in the Abbeyfeale area during the abortive rising of 1848, was a close relative of the Leahys of his time and forebear of our benefactors.

In each company area we constructed hideouts or dumps where all guns and ammunition were stored. The quartermaster in each company was responsible for their maintenance and kept a list of all weapons under his control. The overall control was in the hands of the battalion quartermaster. He, as well as being responsible for all monies collected, had authority in 1920–1921 to issue cigarettes, boots and socks for those "on the run", in poor circumstances.

When searching for arms we got a good supply of shotguns and cartridges from friendly people. In safe houses in our battalion area we converted our cartridges into carrying buckshot instead of the usual shot used for the shooting of wild fowl, rabbits and foxes. To keep these guns and cartridges safe from damp and the guns cleaned and oiled entailed constant attention from each company quartermaster. Our dugouts to hide these weapons had to be lined with strong timber or metal to keep them in good condition. Sometimes we used haybarns as these were really safe and dry and provided a near perfect cover for our purpose. We were short of revolvers and only had a small supply of rifles. In raids for arms we missed a few rifles and Webley revolvers in the possession of ex-army officers. Unfortunately the British authorities had a record of such weapons in the possession of these people and on a couple of occasions forestalled us in securing these guns under our very eyes. In our searches for arms we approached the homes of individuals hostile to us with wariness and due regard for our lives.

In April of this year the police barracks in all country areas were evacuated. The Constabulary moved into the towns for safety owing to the danger, now evident, that if left isolated they'd be practically sitting ducks for the I.R.A. We all rejoiced at this withdrawal as now extensive areas would be free from their surveillance. Immediately on their withdrawal orders were received from G.H.Q. to burn all the buildings lately occupied by them.

In pursuance of this order all evacuated buildings throughout the country, numbering nine hundred, were burned simultaneously on the same night. In discussing this order in my native parish, where a fine building was occupied by them for many years, my comrades and myself decided to hold a *céilí* and a night of frolic and fun in it before it would go up in flames. So we did, to the great enjoyment of all, we lightheartedly danced, courted some nice girl of transient interest "till the dawn of the morning".

Next night I secured some petrol in tins at the creamery nearby. Assisted by some of the boys, I sprinkled petrol all over the floors, and standing at the exit for safety, ignited the petrol. It was my first contact with inflammable liquid and I felt frightened at its explosive speed as it ignited. So vanished before our eyes one hated symbol of English rule.

This was a period of responsibility for me as Battalion O/C. It entailed all the necessary work to try to perfect our force in military exercises, organisation and equipment, with limited means. It entailed many council meetings at battalion and brigade headquarters as well as attending company parades. Disputes also had to be settled as best one could at various courts martial. Protection had to be provided for our Sinn Féin courts and their decisions carried out. I also had the task of organising the Cumann na mBan with the assistance of Nurse Agnes O'Sullivan, Abbeyfeale. She was then appointed in charge of this body and saw to their training until July 1921. Now side by side with all this constant work of trying to improve our military usefulness I still had no idle time at home on the farm. I had to look after the stock, bring provisions to feed my aunt and myself from the local shop, visit my father, mother and sister Mary, in the old home where I was born. The old workman, Jack Wrenn, came to help me out when I was hard pressed. I feel grieved to say that I got no sympathy at home for all I did and never, I sadly relate, did I receive it until the troubles were all over.

Things had their lighter side too. On Sunday afternoons I attended the crossroad dance a few miles away over the mountains. Relaxed there and in the company of local boys and nice girls, enjoyment was to be had. In youth nothing except terrible worry or death has any impact and then only for a short while. This was an exciting time in Ireland. Things of great import were then happening that changed the lives of many.

Our house in Killaculleen was practically the centre and headquarters of our battalion. To it came Sean Finn, our Brigadier, and various officers from time to time. Abbeyfeale, though nominally being headquarters, had no significance at that period so that it was no surprise to me to see Sean Finn, Garrett McAuliffe and some brigade officers arrive one evening in a couple of trap cars. With them were four strangers whom Sean introduced to me as Sean Treacy, Dan Breen, Seamus Robinson and Sean Hogan. I knew immediately that they were wanted men "on the run", and also the cause. In fact the whole country was resounding from the news of the daring rescue of Sean Hogan at Knocklong. Dan Breen was a very sick man from bullet wounds he received near his shoulder. Sean Treacy too was ill from a wound across his neck. My aunt and myself got a couple of beds ready for them, placing their arms within reach. On the departure of Sean Finn and his companions I alerted some of our Volunteer officers to guard against surprise.

I think my aunt received a severe shock as she viewed these men, armed with automatic long-barrelled pistols and bombs. It was then she realised the seriousness of the business we were engaged in and when we were alone she scolded me about the danger we stood in. Early the next day Dr. Eddie Harnett, my first cousin, came to attend the wounded men. He had been notified of their whereabouts and having already attended them at Kennedy's, near Newcastle West, shortly after Knocklong, knew exactly their progress towards recovery. Dan Breen was very ill for some days and vomited a good deal. Sean Treacy made light of his dangerous wound and was most concerned over Breen's condition. They stayed in our house for two weeks and as Dan improved they rambled with me over the roads and fields in the neighbourhood. As we chatted together it was apparent to me that henceforth their purpose was to wage war against the enemy at every opportunity. Later events proved this was to be so.

One day as we rambled along the road towards the creamery Treacy stopped at the junction between two roads, both meeting like a V. The point of the V commanded a straight stretch of road with a high hedge on one side and a high bank on the other, and protecting this V formation was an impenetrable hedge and big trees. Sean Treacy was impressed as he viewed the place and thought it made an ideal ambush position. Another afternoon I took them along the river where in seclusion we lazed away a few hours. Dan Breen was interested in fishing and in discussing fishing habits in our locality. I told him about some methods of catching fish practised in our locality. I pointed out to him a plant growing around us which I said when pulled up by the roots, then placed in a strong bag and pounded into pulp, exuded a milky substance extremely poisonous to fish. This bag, when placed in the shallows at the entrance to a large pool, caused the flow of water to release this poisonous substance which was so virulent that it could poison a large number of fish. They were then easily collected as they floated senseless on the surface of the water. Dan was disgusted and did not think very much of such persons. This plant is known locally as "yellow root".

Sean Hogan, then very young, took their serious situation good humouredly though conscious of his rescue from the armed police and of the deaths that had occurred during this bloody operation. I procured a bicycle for him and he and Tommy Leahy (a somewhat kindred spirit) cycled some days on remote mountain roads a few miles away. Peddling along one evening, they came to a lonesome bleak moorland glen with the sombre hills looking down, frowning on them, desolate and dreary. "Well Tom", says Sean, "I would not like to die fighting for Ireland in this place, I don't think it's worth it." Laughing and joking with each other they spent this and other evenings as if they hadn't a care in the world. It is amazing how danger, constant as it was at that time, never prevented any wanted man from sleeping soundly at night, though ever ready to snatch his gun and dash outside at the first alarm.

Our house in Killaculleen was a quarter of a mile in from the road linking Dromcollogher with Abbeyfeale and Newcastle West. It was about eight miles distant from each town, secluded and safe from prying eyes. The neighbours were good and helpful, loyal to the I.R.A. at all times. Sean Treacy was fond of reading and picked out some books from the small store we had in the house to read during his periods of rest and recuperation. Safe as we thought our wanted men to be there was always the danger lurking around. This was brought home to us one evening as Sean Hogan and I were sauntering along the road leading to Abbeyfeale. Near the entrance to the boreen leading to their billet, we saw approaching on a bicycle a man dressed in dark clothes. As he came nearer we recognised him as a policeman. Sean said to me "what will we do? Will we hold him up and disarm him?" We both had guns under our coats and could have done so. Quickly I thought, if we do this the whole place will be searched immediately with dangerous possibilities. So in a few words I whispered to

Sean "don't do anything, let him pass". The policeman, whom I knew from Abbeyfeale barracks, saluted us both on passing and cycled away. By the end of April about a month had passed since the police barracks were burned. Constables, singly, and few in numbers, ventured into the country now and went out on cycling patrols.

This meeting with a police constable, some five miles from his barracks, and the possible consequence put us all on the alert. We decided it might be safer to move someplace else, so we took up our sleeping quarters in a hayshed belonging to a neighbouring farmer. There we had an uneasy sleep. After climbing a ladder onto the hay, tormented by hay insects and the cold at night, rest was almost impossible. At this time I received a warning from a friendly police sergeant named Kearns that a search on a large scale was to take place in our district. As a result I arranged with Tommy Leahy to get a party of armed Volunteers ready with cars (horse traps) to convey our wanted men by night to Knocknagoshel, Co. Kerry. There at the home of the O'Connors, cousins of mine, they would get welcome and protection. We made the journey through byroads to avoid the town of Abbeyfeale. Unfortunately we went astray and one of our party, Danny Curtin, fell off the car (a side car), coming down a steep hill. He suffered a concussion and had to be attended to before we continued our journey. Dawn was breaking (being early summer), and on looking around us we saw to our horror that we were just about to enter the western end of the town. Our road, called Betty Road, joined the main Limerick to Tralee road and at the junction, between both, stood the police barracks, with an unhindered view of both roads. We held a hasty consultation and decided to run the gauntlet and looked to our guns to make ready for possible interception. So, unhurriedly, we passed the back and front of the barracks, our cars rattling over the stony road in the early morning light. Safely past we sighed with relief and muttered silent prayers at our escape from probable death. If the policeman on guard in the barracks saw our approach and alerted the garrison a bloody fight would have taken place.

On the day following our dangerous journey to Knocknagoshel a search was carried out by a large number of military and police a few miles from where I lived. So I parted from Treacy, Breen, Hogan and Robinson, the most wanted young men in Ireland at that time. During their stay in O'Connor's, Tommy Leahy, Jack Aherne and I visited them on two occasions and on our second visit attended a dance in their company at Dinny Leen's farmhouse nearby. Shortly afterwards they left for the home of Jim Colbert in Athea. Subsequently I met them again in Dublin at the public house of Phil Shanahan, in Foley Street. This was some months before Sean Treacy was killed in Talbot Street, in 1920. Sean Hogan was not present at this meeting. My next meeting was a chance encounter in Dublin with Seamus Robinson and Slope Reidy of Rathkeale in O'Connell Street. On coming upstairs at Phil Shanahan's, with my companions, I remember that Sean Treacy was seated at a large table, writing, and on the table was displayed, for instant use, some large automatic pistols and Mills bombs. On entering the room Seamus Robinson pulled up from the leg of his trousers a long Parabellum. That was the last time I saw Sean Treacy alive.

During the year 1919 meetings, assemblies and sports were held all over the country to further the aims of Sinn Féin and for the collection of funds. Most of these gatherings were proclaimed by the military authorities. Some were in selected places in defiance of the British; one was held near Dromcollogher, in a wood. It was addressed by William Cosgrave, Minister for Home Affairs in the first Dáil. It was attended by hundreds of people. They all assembled in this wood secretly and a decoy party prepared an alternative site in the town, watched by police and soldiers. It did not dawn on the authorities that they were the victims of a hoax. It was a day of great excitement and tension in this battle of wits between Sinn Féin and the Crown Forces. It was regarded as a special event locally and won applause from enthusiastic supporters.

Volunteers and hundreds of people, young and old, organised and held these meetings in all districts. I attended, in the local towns, several of these proclaimed gatherings. One great gathering near Mt. Collins village was held in a field, and was addressed by Professor Stockley of University College Cork. Local priests were there and prominent amongst the clergy was Father Lynch, C.C, Brosna. Our Sinn Féin T.D., Con Collins, gave a spirited address. The meeting had a hurried ending on the arrival of a large company of soldiers and police. The dispersing crowd of adults and children streaming to the village were confronted by the armed forces of the Crown, hurrying up a high road to stop by force any attempt to hold a meeting. In a solid phalanx they marched through the crowd with rifles at the ready to the abandoned field and took possession of the improvised platform. It was but a poor consolation for their long journey from their barracks at Ballymullan, Tralee. At night in local schools, after these proclaimed gatherings on Sunday afternoons, enjoyable concerts and dances were held where rebellious ballads were sung, recitations given and the inevitable dance took place. The dance was fast and furious and many's the young boy and girl, often meeting for the first time under the night's enchantment, pledged hasty promises of future meetings and made vows (sometimes unfulfilled) in the exciting atmosphere of the night, engendered by time and place.

It was a well-organised business at that time to try and use every tactic to fool the police and military when holding Sinn Féin assemblies and political meetings. In our parish one Sunday afternoon we arranged to hold our meeting about a mile away from the usual place, a field near the church. We sent our fife and drum band to an eminence, plainly in view for all to see. In a field across a little river directly opposite this a half a mile away we held a large enthusiastic meeting. Some prominent members of the I.R.A. and Sinn Féin organisations stayed near the church in full view of the police who knew them well. The military and police arrived in force and marched up and down the road for some time before realising the deception that was being practiced on them. The presence of such prominent Republicans at the recognised meeting place deceived them for a time until the martial music, played by the band, and the waving of flags on a hillside some distance away alerted them to the deception practised on them. Contrary to their usual habit of breaking up these gatherings they remained inactive on this occasion and after a time withdrew, frustrated in their attempt in enforcing the proclamation prohibiting such gatherings.

The Dáil Éireann Loan, launched by the National Assembly all over the country and in America, was a wonderful success. A considerable amount of money (around a quarter of a million pounds) was subscribed in Ireland. This, with the money received in the U.S.A., was of considerable assistance to our infant parliament and played a big part in the disse-mination of truthful news to acquaint the world regarding the state of the country at that time. Here in our parish the people generously subscribed £240 to the loan. The bigger farmers subscribed £5 each, then considered a large sum of money. Without exception, all paid generously according to their means, from the humble labourer to the most well-off. Though some did not agree with the Sinn Féin programme they still contributed, though maybe grudgingly.

We made a house-to-house collection all over the parish and sometimes had to justify our programme by cogent arguments in its defence. On one occasion, the creamery manager, Edward Farrell, and myself were collecting. We had an argu-ment with a substantial farmer (a returned Yank). He could not be convinced that persons like us, of no means or property, and classified by him as men of straw, could better the country politically or otherwise. Well, he lived to see the outcome of our combined efforts. I never met him afterwards to hear his views and comments on those glorious and tragic years culminating in our uneasy peace. I expect he believed that we should have left things very well alone.

On our collections we were welcomed with extreme good will in some houses. Some families were really patriotic in their outlook and from past association which they had with the national movement down through the years were proud and glad to help once again in the advancement and success of Sinn Féin and the I.R.A. I can still remember the generous meal that awaited us at the home of the Leahy's of Ballycommane. Molly Leahy overwhelmed us to the extent to which a generous heart like hers contributed to the loaded table of good things placed before us. All this was done in our honour simply because we represented in our day a link in the chain extending back to former resistance against tyranny witnessed in the days of her youth. My companion was usually Tom Leahy, and being a relative of theirs was doubly welcome, as he bore their name too. He also had inherited from his ancestors a record for rebellion against the established order.

During this period in rural Ireland and indeed in most cities and towns, English law no longer functioned. Their courts were mostly silent and abandoned. Sinn Féin courts took over the maintenance of law and order and here all brought their grievances to be settled cheaply and satisfactorily. The legal profession supported these courts everywhere, defended their clients or otherwise as was their custom formerly before magistrates or county court judges. Of course, the parish court was the centre of interest for all local people. Here the president was usually the local curate or some well-to-do intelligent farmer. Attending these courts to listen to the various arguments between litigants came a great number of people, really to be amused, get a good laugh and to have something to talk about afterwards. The district court, being a step higher in the legal profession, was where more serious cases were heard as well as appeals from the findings of the parish court. Here you'd find the local solicitors with their training in the intricacies of the law propounding their interpretation of the case for or against some appellant or defendant.

Our parish court held its sessions in a room attached to the shop of William Aherne, who was at that time Treasurer of the local Sinn Féin cumann. Our local Catholic curate, Father Michael Twomey, was president of the court; generally his decision was accepted by the parties in dispute. Sometimes this decision was ignored and it was the duty of the local

I.R.A. to see that it was carried out. This caused ill-feeling and hatred, I am sorry to say, in some persons. The I.R.A. men involved in some cases were never forgiven though they acted as impartial instruments of justice. I got directly involved in one particular case in carrying out the decision of our parish court and the people whose case went against them defied our endeavours for a peaceful settlement. We had to resort to strong arm tactics to force them to accept this settlement in justification of the findings of the parish court and in upholding its decision. The County Court Judge, Mr. E. McElligott, appointed by the Free State government in 1924–25 to investigate the legality of all these Sinn Féin court decisions for Kerry, Limerick and Clare, brought in a verdict in favour of the terms laid down by our parish court in this dispute.

Father Michael Twomey was a vigorous supporter of the methods used in the implementation of the parish court's decisions and was foremost as leader locally in furthering the national aims, civil and military. He was a fine, tall, athletic man, in his late twenties. He had an exhilarating and exciting effect on his young impressionable audiences. He could get them to accept implicitly, by the sheer force of his personality and impassioned speech, his direction in carrying out his will on almost anything pertaining to Sinn Féin and kindred organisations. He believed in justice for the people and would go to extremes to attain it. He did not believe that cool, calm methods were the best to attain this and his nature being impetuous, sustained by courage and generosity, brooked no delay in the settlement of local wrongs brought before him in his capacity as president of the Sinn Féin court and outside it.

Our parish priest, Father Hartigan, one of the conservative cautious school, then very much in evidence, could find no common ground on which to agree with Father Twomey. The result was friction between them on matters, especially local ones, as here the direct methods of one clashed with the cautious old-fashioned opinion of the other. The parish priest, of course, considered by the people to be the father and advisor of his flock, was generally accepted as such. He took

a dim view of the new movement, risen like a phoenix almost
overnight, like an avalanche to overwhelm existing and seemingly impregnable forces up till then our masters.

The tension existing between them at that time came out
in the open over the case I have mentioned earlier. To the
amazement of most people attending a public meeting during
the early part of 1919, Father Twomey, in the course of his
address said: "Referring to the business of calling together a
meeting of Sinn Féin followers to emphasize the importance
of what the issue was, namely, could it be tolerated that any
litigant acted in open defiance of the legitimate court of the
land, established by Dáil Éireann? Further, that in the spring
of that year some got protection from the R.I.C. in the form
of armed guards for their person and property." These were
withdrawn at the end of April, 1919 and then replaced by local
vigilantes until pressure by the I.R.A. caused them to be
disbanded. Of course the parish priest accepted the authority
of the then fast disintegrating British establishment and gave
his support accordingly. Father Twomey, stirred by our
delighted applause, proclaimed that our parish priest's idea of
an Irish Republic did not go beyond the limits of his farm and
that it was, apart from his pastoral duties, the place where his
only interest lay—in the pleasure he got in looking at his cattle
each day with loving gaze and watching nature at work during
the passing years. Father Twomey, defiant and eloquent, described the parish priest's image in the then existing situation
as follows: "Father Hartigan's Irish Republic is thirty acres of
Glebe land, bounded on the west by Patsy Tom and on the
east by Tom Larry." "That", said he, "is Father Hartigan's
Irish Republic!"

One of the men forced "on the run" during 1919–20 was
Sean Brouder, the editor of a paper called the *Weekly Observer*.
It was published and printed at the premises owned by him
in Maiden Street, Newcastle West. It had a good circulation
all over County Limerick. His business included printing posters,
announcing auctions, meetings, assemblies and festivals. Many
a journey I paid to his place of business from 1917 to 1920 to

get these assembly posters printed as well as dance cards for a céilídhe we organised. He was a dedicated man to this work and paid the usual price in 1920 when his office works was raided. The police and soldiers destroyed all the printing machinery with sledge-hammers and also destroyed papers and literature. This destruction of his livelihood, as well as danger to his liberty, forced him to take to the hills of the West. His home in Newcastle West where he lived with his sister Babe was always open to the "boys". Many a rebel song was sung around the fire there at night and plans discussed to frustrate and defeat their enemy's tactics. Poor Babe had not much peace after Sean's flight to the country. She was subjected to nocturnal raids by police and soldiers on her privacy and home.

During 1919 a surprise raid by the British forces was made at the home of Denis Aherne, a section commander in our local company I.R.A. He was in the kitchen when the military were espied coming up a short boreen leading to the house. Immediately, as he ran out, fire was opened on him by the Crown Forces. Miraculously he escaped as he ran up the open hillside for a hundred yards or so, then jumped over a fence which gave him protection, enabling him to make good his escape. We all wondered at the raid but came to the conclusion that the police must have come by information from some source to cause them to believe that he was a prominent I.R.A. man. This information to the police was correct so far as that Dinny Aherne was a cousin of Con Collins, T.D., a wanted man. In his own right he was a determined opponent of British rule and ready to do anything to bring about its downfall. Alas, death intervened shortly after this occasion, bringing to an end his patriotic efforts as a soldier of Ireland.

During 1919 we raided the homes of R.I.C. men on leave. We usually left them in no uncertain mind as to what would happen to them if they did not resign from the force. Our appearance at night was rather terrifying for them and their relatives as we burst into some remote farmhouse, threatening most dire consequences as we pointed our guns menacingly at some unprotected policeman. It was amazing to realise how far apart some of these policemen, reared amongst us, were from us in those troubled days. Some few realised the seriousness of their position in relation to the national effort. This led to the resignations in various parts of Ireland of young active R.I.C. men, disgusted at the work they unwillingly did.

As the year of 1919 drew to a close, clashes and open war developed between our forces and the police. Barracks were attacked, some captured. Police were attacked in several places and death resulted on both sides. In November, I visited relatives living in Dublin. An uncle of mine, Denis Mulcahy, who was a sportsman in his time, gave me a suitcase of cartridges to bring home to West Limerick. He accompanied me to Kingsbridge Station and with my treasonable goods saw me safely aboard the train. On our arrival at Kingsbridge we were in a nervous state on espying the whole place swarming with military and police.

Sauntering unconcernedly past the ticket checker at the gate, in trepidation, we moved down the platform in a leisurely fashion until I entered a compartment filled with soldiers belonging to some British regiment. There I took a seat amongst them after placing my bag of cartridges on the rack above my head. My uncle Denis, glad to be rid of me and my incriminating suitcase, departed after a hasty good-bye. He was really a good cover for me, as he had the military bearing of a retired army officer. He was a fine tall man with the appearance that goes with military service. His tremendous moustache, erect carriage and cultured accent proclaimed to strangers that here was one of Britain's old reliables. In fact, in his young days, he served in "The South Irish Horse", a cavalry regiment disbanded at the start of the war. In any event I brought home this shotgun ammunition which was so badly required safely to my native place.

CHAPTER IV.

THE BLACK AND TANS, 1920–1921.

During 1919, and up to the Truce in 1921, a special effort was made to perfect our intelligence system. I spent much time in our battalion area organising the intelligence into a near perfect one. From my knowledge of available material, I put in charge Edward Leahy, a creamery manager of unquestionable integrity, as Battalion O/C Intelligence. He had under him the company intelligence officers in each district in the battalion area. These were to report immediately on any suspicious movements of enemy forces, and in particular were to keep a close look out for suspected spies. In addition we had the wholehearted co-operation of Cumann na mBan, and of various civilians who could move without suspicion among the military and police. All strangers coming into the district were closely watched, and their movements reported.

At this period (1919–1920) young men were continually joining our battalion area, seeking refuge. They came from various counties, were "on the run", and had moved from company to company. They were usually vouched for by officers of their respective areas, but it was an arrangement that carried definite risks of infiltration by the enemy. It happened, in fact, that in this way a dangerous spy infiltrated our own ranks. It took some months before this was discovered.

My first contact with this person was late in the autumn of 1919. He brought with him credentials that convinced all the I.R.A. officers in West Limerick and East Kerry of his genuineness as an I.R.A. man "on the run" from his enemies.

He was introduced to me by Sean Finn, O/C Brigade, by a name (Peadar Clancy) that was subsequently found to be fictitious, and so I shall refer to him as "A" for the purpose of this narrative. He said he was from Co. Tipperary. I myself and two officers of my battalion were his companions from then on in the activities in which we were engaged, generally raiding for arms. On one such occasion, when we encountered strong opposition, I noticed that "A" was very aggressive and brandished his revolver.

He stayed in my house for approximately one month (late 1919), and was then taken to Knocknagoshel, and from there to a district adjoining Castleisland. Prior to his departure he joined in a lunch offered by our local curate, Fr. Twomey, at an Abbeyfeale hotel. Here "A" surprised me by taking rather too much spirits, a thing foreign to the habits of I.R.A. men "on the run". He also engaged in a flow of very unsuitable conversation, especially in the presence of so saintly a priest. I felt disgusted and succeeded in bringing our meeting to as early an end as possible. But no suspicion as to "A's" real role ever entered my mind. I was to meet him again in the spring of 1920, in completely different circumstances.

Early in March, 1920, our intelligence received information that led to the arrest of "A" as a suspected spy. He was at that time living among I.R.A. families in Kerry. I was notified by the Brigade O/C Intelligence, to be prepared to find accommodation for "A" and to keep him under strict guard, night and day. Needless to say, I felt somewhat put out at meeting him again in this manner. Four senior officers of the East Kerry Brigade brought him to West Limerick on a night in March 1920. On receipt of the information that had led to his arrest they had searched him, and were astonished at finding a large sum of money hidden in a pocket under his armpit. They also found on him documents written in code, which they were unable to decipher.

On arrival of the prisoner in West Limerick he was lodged and closely guarded in a remote farmhouse occupied by an old lady and a farm workman, neither of whom had a great

welcome for us. Our Brigade O/C and Vice O/C and other
officers, including Sean Hogan of Knocklong Rescue fame,
came to see the prisoner next day and questioned him at
length, and discussed what should be done with him. It was
arranged that he should be court-martialled. The court martial
was to be made up of the principal officers of the brigade
staff, together with some senior officers from the East Kerry
Brigade, and Con Collins, a Sinn Féin T.D., then "on the
run" in the area.

Acting on instructions, I made arrangements with the
occupants of another farmhouse living nearby to provide their
sitting room for the court which was to be held there. It took
some days before the court was ready to sit. In the meantime
the prisoner acted as if nothing of importance was happening.
We all tried to act naturally, as naturally as we could in the
strained circumstances. "A" got ample supplies of cigarettes;
we played cards with him, and accompanied him on walking
exercises outside the house. He seemed calm except for one
little incident.

This incident was caused by a magpie which came each
morning and perched on the window sill outside the bedroom
where "A" slept. The magpie would persistently peck away
at the glass of the window in the early morning light. "Do
you know", said "A" to me, referring to the magpie's strange
behaviour, "I don't like it, and it portends no good." Stranger
still, the magpie came to the window only while "A" slept in
the house.

The day of the trial eventually came. Of the seven officers
forming the court, one was selected to act in "A's" defence;
another was selected as prosecuting officer. The prisoner stren-
uously denied that he was a spy who had infiltrated the I.R.A.
After several hours deliberation, no verdict was reached; but
the court decided to sit again if any new evidence should come
to light. There was of course the matter of the documents in
code. Here the prisoner gave us no help, and kept a shut mouth.
I suppose if we were bad enough to have tortured or terrorised
him he might have spoken, but such were not our methods.

The court officers decided to send the coded documents to the I.R.A. staff headquarters in Cork. There, on the documents being deciphered, it was established beyond all doubt that "A" was an enemy agent engaged in espionage. When confirmation of this reached West Limerick, it was arranged to call the court together again. Meantime, "A" seemed to be getting more and more restless. This was particularly noticeable on an occasion when only one guard had charge of him. The surprising thing is that he didn't suddenly try to overpower the guard and make a bolt for it.

The unanimous verdict of the court on its second sitting was that "A" was guilty, and he was sentenced to death by firing squad. The execution was to be carried out in the early morning hours of the next day. Scouts and guards were placed in a wide circle round the lonely field where the execution was to take place. With few feelings of sorrow I now saw the prisoner being driven off in a pony and trap between two guards. Fully realising now his terrible predicament, and visibly trembling, he clutched his Rosary in his hands. Near the place of execution, a priest heard his confession; then he shook hands with his executioners and admitted his crime.

Returning in the early hours of the morning, the two guards tumbled into the bed in which the executed man had slept during his imprisonment. As they were settling down to sleep, the front door gave a very loud bang as a result of a sudden gust of high wind. Immediately they jumped out of bed, holding drawn revolvers, startled by this unexpected alarm, and ready for the worst. It was a false alarm of course, but it underlines the frightful tension under which men lived, even slept, at that time.

Early in May, 1920, a meeting between the officers of the West Limerick and East Limerick Brigades of the I.R.A. was held at the home of Mike Cregan, Monagae. A long discussion took place as to the feasibility of attacking either the Newcastle West or Kilmallock R.I.C. barracks, and eventually it was decided that the attack would be made against the Kilmallock barracks. Kilmallock, one of the strongest police barracks in the south of Ireland, had been bravely but vainly attacked by the Fenians in 1867, and it was felt that its destruction at this stage of the War of Independence in 1920 would have a demoralising effect on the forces of the British Crown.

The fateful night of the attack arrived, and West Limerick Volunteers, who had been previously selected to participate in the fight, met at the home of Mrs. MacInerney, Camas, Monagae. Tommy Leahy, Jack Aherne and myself attended together with Sean Finn, O/C West Limerick Brigade, I.R.A., Garrett McAuliffe, Vice O/C, C. Cregan, Larry MacNamee and Jimmy Roche, as well as a number of other Volunteers.

The number of Volunteers present was far in excess of the number the West Limerick Brigade was to have supplied— the latter number being decided by the number of rifles and shotguns available. The problem of picking the men who were to go to Kilmallock was left to Brigade O/C, Sean Finn, who chose ten men who were armed with either rifles or shotguns. Neither I, Tommy Leahy nor Jack Aherne were among those selected. Some motor cars were assembled to take the fighting men to Kilmallock. I know that I got two cars, one from Michael O'Mahony, creamery manager, Devon Rd., the other from Richard Roche, Meenahela creamery. Larry MacNamee drove the O'Mahony car.

After seeing our comrades drive off towards Kilmallock on their fateful journey, we returned home by Glenquin Castle, and sat for a while by the fireside, speculating on the outcome of the fierce fight we knew was by then in progress in Kilmallock. Down there in the central plain of Limerick men were engaged in a deadly struggle for possession of that barracks, long a symbol of British dominance. We had to wait for the light of the next morning to get any news from our comrades about the outcome of the fight.

I was up early, and had occasion to go out to the public road, which was connected with my home by a long boreen. I was on the road only a few minutes when I was surprised to see two motor cars arrive. They stopped immediately when they saw me, and from both cars several armed men jumped out. In one car I noticed a young man lying on a stretcher, with a young nurse in uniform sitting beside him. The young man, who was dead, was Captain Liam Scully, B.A., and he had been shot through the neck in the fight. The young nurse was Miss O'Sullivan, who had rendered first aid to the wounded Scully when he was brought into a house near the barracks after being shot.

As for the fight itself, it had lasted for six hours, and was the fiercest such engagement of the War of Independence. The garrison in the barracks, consisting of two sergeants and eighteen constables, put up a heroic defence, even after their fortress began to collapse in flames above their heads. At that stage they retreated into a strongly built outhouse from where they kept up the fight, refusing to surrender. Two of their comrades perished in the flames. The main outcome of the fight, as far as the I.R.A. was concerned, was that they had succeeded in completely destroying the barracks, for long considered an impregnable fortress.

But to return to the scene after the armed men had left their cars that morning near my home. Among them I recognised Sean Finn, Garrett McAuliffe and Larry MacNamee. Sean Finn introduced me to the others, who included Michael Brennan, Tom Malone (alias Sean Forde), and Patrick Clancy. Sean consulted me as to the safest place near at hand where we could leave Liam Scully's remains. I suggested a farmhouse, O'Gorman's, near my own home, but even more secluded, and further too from the road. In fact, this particular farmhouse was at least three-quarters of a mile from the road—the Dromcollogher–Abbeyfeale road—and had the added advantage of being occupied only by a caretaker, William Long, and his two sons.

As we moved slowly down the rambling boreen to our destination, I heard a vivid description of the fight from the boys who, only a few hours before, had been engaged in that desperate struggle. On reaching the house, I explained our business to the occupants. Placing our sad burden on a bed in the sitting room, a meal was got ready in the kitchen. The fighting men then sought some hours sleep on the few beds in the place. Meantime I went home and made contact with Tommy Leahy and Jack Aherne and we arranged for armed guards to be placed around the house where the Volunteers were with their dead comrade.

In an outhouse in O'Gorman's farmyard, Con Kiely of Strand, with a helper, made a crude plain coffin of deal boards. I owned a Volunteer officer's uniform with a Sam Browne belt, and in these we dressed the remains, which were then laid in the coffin, with a guard of honour standing at attention as he lay in state on a big timber bed.

The sunny afternoon drew to a close, and after dark a party of Volunteer officers arrived from East Limerick. The caretaker of Templeglantine churchyard was notified that a burial was to take place during the night. Family burial plots occupied all the graveyard area, and there was no vacant space; but one man eventually gave permission to have a grave opened in this burial space.

In sad procession we bore on our shoulders Liam Scully's mortal remains from O'Gormans to 'Glantine cemetery on a fine balmy summer's night. We gave him a full military funeral, as befitted a brave young man. Father Dick McCarthy of Ballyhahill performed the religious ceremony, and an oration was delivered by one of the East Limerick Brigade officers. Amongst those in attendance at the burial was the dead man's brother, Bertie Scully, all the way from Caragh Lake in Kerry.

In due course the East Limerick men returned home across country from the funeral, fully armed; and when they arrived at the home of John Lynch at Tankardstown, between Bruree and Kilmallock, the idea occurred to one of their leaders, Donncadh O'Hannigan, that in view of what they had done they should form a small permanent fighting force that could devote its whole time to carrying war to the British forces who, against the declared will of the Irish people, held their land in subjection by violence and force. And so was born the famous Flying Column of the East Limerick Brigade, I.R.A., the first such flying column to be formed during the War of Independence.

On 5 June 1920 the Brosna police barracks was attacked
by the I.R.A. Approximately twelve boys from Tournafulla,
'Glantine, Abbeyfeale and Monegae took part along with the
Kerry I.R.A. They included Tommy Leahy, Jack Aherne,
Paddy Buckley, Ned Harnett (The Landlord), Paddy Mulcahy,
Con and Ned Cregan of Monegae, Jim Roche of 'Glantine,
Ger. Kiely, Daniel Riordan (car driver), Willie McAuliffe (lorry
driver), Tom Boucher, Paddy Aherne and myself.

We assembled at Knocknadiha crossroads on Saturday
evening, 4 June 1920. There we distributed the rifles, taken after
the Kilmallock barrack attack; also some shotguns and ammunition for the rifles and guns. We divided our party between
the motor car and lorry and drove up the road until we reached
the Limerick/Kerry border around 10 o'clock p.m. We hid
our motor transport in a yard near Mt. Collins; there a guide
met us and took us up hilly fields towards Brosna where we
passed by the creamery and up a high road into an elevated
field (owned by Sonny McAuliffe). Here was assembled a body
of I.R.A. men under the command of Humphrey Murphy,
Commdt. East Kerry Brigade. Included in his force were Tom
and Charlie Daly, Jerry O'Leary, Dan McCarthy, Tadg Matt
O'Connor, Battalion O/C., Dave and Ned McCarthy, and
Tom McEllistrim of Ballymacelligot. Then the officers discussed
the plan of attack, dividing the I.R.A. into units of about half
a dozen or so, each under an officer with specific directions
as to the positions to be occupied and the method of attack.
All moved off at midnight and our boys from Limerick under
my command took possession of a small house at the rear of
the barracks, barricaded the small windows with anything
available and fired from there at loopholes in the iron windows
of the besieged fortress. I myself with Tom Leahy, Paddy
Buckley and some others occupied a position fronting the
heavily guarded building and fired at the loopholes in the iron
shutters. One needed to be a sniper to do so, and here Paddy
Buckley with his skill with a rifle was invaluable.

The Kerrymen had by now taken up their allotted places
in the scheme of attack; some faced the front from houses in

the Square, others tried their skill on the roof after mounting a high ladder placed against the gable wall where there was no window, and they smashed the roof with heavy hammers. Explosives were used in the form of blasting powder enclosed in two iron cylinders placed in the boxes of a farm cart with fuse attached. Both cylinders were tied to each other by strong rope then thrown across the ridge tiles and dropped into the holes broken in the roof. When the fuses were lit things didn't work as planned as the police heard the noise over their heads and then started firing through the slates close to both gables. This became too dangerous for the roof breakers who eventually had to withdraw. The rifle fire and exploding grenades made the night resound to a hideous volume of noise re-echoing back from the surrounding hills. In lulls in the firing we could distinctly hear a melodian being played and shouts from the beleaguered garrison of "Come on the rainbow chasers". Our boys loudly replied with shouts of "Come out ye whores of bastards!", as tempers rose. All this time the hiss of the deadly bullets, as they passed close by us, was a reminder of the deadly menace their message conveyed.

Frequently Verey lights were sent up during the night to summon aid from the garrisons of Abbeyfeale and Castleisland. We guarded ourselves by placing armed parties on all roads leading to Brosna and the two towns mentioned and had cut all telegraph wires in the district. Our protecting outposts near Abbeyfeale and Castleisland came in contact with enemy forces who hastened to assist the Brosna police. Their action saved us as otherwise we in our withdrawal would have been attacked by them.

Near Abbeyfeale the police had to retreat to their barracks carrying their wounded with them but continued firing at the party who had ambushed them. Military from Ballymullan, Tralee were delayed when sniped on by a party of I.R.A. who were protecting their comrades on some high hills east of Castleisland—this gave the Kerrymen time to retreat and evade the military. On a glorious Sunday morning in June, after five hours of continuous fighting, we were ordered to leave our positions and assemble at the crossroads beside the creamery. We withdrew in broad daylight and had miraculous escapes from sniper fire in our retreat.

At the creamery we had a meal of bread and cheese and a short discussion on our unavailing efforts. We then said goodbye to our Kerry comrades. Hastening over the fields we crossed the Feale river at Mt. Collins to join our transport. Unfortunately the motor car refused to budge so we left Daniel Riordan and a couple of our party to help him start it. The rest of us got on the lorry driven by Wm. McAuliffe and with our guns and depleted ammunition reached Tournafulla without incident. Tom Leahy took charge of the rifles, etc. and with helpers put them in a safe place near the Cork border. The others dispersed to 'Glantine and Monegae on bicycles and the lorry was driven off in the direction of Abbeyfeale.

Later that morning I attended nine o'clock Mass and as I was standing beside the church chatting to some neighbours I was alarmed when I saw two motor cars approach from the direction of Newcastle West on their way to Brosna. Both cars had armed police in them and sitting beside the driver in the first car was an inspector whom I recognised. Our men at Mt. Collins repairing their car had just completed the job and were about to drive onto the road when they spied the two cars approaching. They stayed put and thanked their lucky stars that the police whom they saw pass quickly by never saw them. When the enemy had vanished from sight they quickly drove off and their car behaved alright, bringing them safely to Tournafulla and finally to Devon Road where Dan Riordan drove it into the premises of the owner, Michael O'Mahony, creamery manager.

These ordeals and escapes were the hazards of war. The barracks in Brosna was ably defended by Sergeant Coughlin with twelve constables. The I.R.A. suffered no casualties either at Brosna or Abbeyfeale.

"Sean Forde" came to my home one evening to collect the carbines, rifles and ammunition on loan to us after Kilmallock and Brosna. Captain Tommy Leahy, with a couple of

Volunteers, collected these armaments and brought them to Kelly's farmhouse, a few yards distant from my home. There they were counted and examined, so that a correct tally be made. Of course the rifle ammunition was depleted owing to its expenditure against Brosna barracks.

While this was taking place one of the scouts on a lookout point near the public road, about four hundred yards away, saw the lights of a truck approaching in the distance and assumed it to be a Crossley tender with an armed party of military. He at once assumed that they were on a search, or raid, and that Kelly's would be a likely place for them to search as well as my home. On the alarm being raised, the guns were removed in a great hurry by Tom Leahy, "Sean Forde" and Denny Wrenn. In running from the house, the bandoliers carrying the cartridges were forgotten in the scramble to get away. They ran down the garden path, giving entrance to a high sloping field, and in the darkness of the night ran into a field of barbed wire and got caught in it. On hearing a voice behind them calling, Tommy Leahy recognised it as being Mrs. Kelly's. Going back to investigate he discovered that she had collected the ammunition into her apron and was now hurrying with it to our aid. After all, guns without feeding would not be much use at any time.

In a short time the alarm had subsided, as this truck or Crossley tender passed by without stopping. Returning to the house with their valuable guns and ammunition, "Sean Forde" after a hasty meal loaded them into his motor car in the rear behind the front seats; covering his valuable cargo with some coats. Then taking his seat at the driving wheel, with an automatic pistol and some grenades beside him, drove off for East Limerick which he reached safely.

Our Captain, Tommy Leahy, Jack Aherne, Adjt. and myself were discussing things one evening, seated on sugan chairs and toasting our feet before a turf fire in our kitchen. My aunt was just on her way to bed, when suddenly we were jumping out of our chairs; our calm shattered by a loud explosion in our midst. Jack Aherne had his two feet planted firmly on the hob for comfort. He started, during our talk, to take out his revolver from its holster, twirled it about, and made a plaything out of it. In doing this, unconsciously he placed his right forefinger on the trigger, gave it a squeeze and bang went the shot, to be imbedded in the chimney wall between his feet. Talk of a fright! It caused my aunt to nearly collapse and our friend Jack to get paler than he usually was. Tom and myself, I can tell you, gave Jack a piece of our minds. We were getting used to hazards of this kind and before the fight was over several of the boys "on the run" lost their lives in accidents caused by explosions and gunfire.

My Aunt Mary was at this period used to seeing guns, grenades and rifle bullets thrown around in the kitchen and bedrooms. Usually these weapons were kept close by their owners. Some never were without them, especially revolvers, carried in holsters strapped to their right leg. When finally the war was over, I personally felt undressed without a weapon by my side. Others told me the same story: such was the magnetic attraction of their possession, that one was in a state of near mesmerism or fascination. Possession of a gun gave a feeling of confidence as one faced danger, and equality was established against odds in the hit-and-run warfare at that time.

One evening, early in July, my sister Mary visited us from the old home in Knocknadiha. She came principally to bake some bread, as there were always hungry I.R.A. boys around to eat some. Whilst cleaning the rooms and seeing to the bed sheets etc., she felt it would warm up the parlour if she lit a fire in the grate. So with a basket of turf and some bogdale sticks beside her, she finished her work and was about to set it alight, when as an afterthought she looked under the grate to see if any ashes remained from the previous fire. Poking about with a little shovel, she brought out some object, shaped like a goose egg and dark in colour. Calling me to identify it, I, immediately on inspection, knew that it was a Mills bomb, probably placed there by one of the boys and forgotten about. I shuddered to think what would be the outcome, if a blazing fire on top of it exploded the grenade with people sitting close around. This is probably what would have happened as the heat must certainly have released the detonator or ignited the inflammable substance the bomb contained.

I received a dispatch towards the middle of July to attend an important meeting of the brigade staff to consider a directive from G.H.Q. to train and equip a Flying Column. Accordingly all the men "on the run" in our area were ordered to meet at a farmhouse, "Scanlon's" Dirreen, Athea, on 20 July. These included officers and all men at that time who were whole-time Volunteers, especially those from the towns, who could not possibly remain at home only to be arrested by the police.

Approximately thirty-five men were selected, with Garrett McAuliffe, Vice Commandant, Brigade as O/C Column and Michael Colbert, Captain as his assistant. These men were armed with rifles, revolvers and explosives. Brigade O/C, Sean Finn and his staff, were to remain with the column and have authority to plan and prepare in detail future activities against the Crown Forces to be carried out by the column. The staff was responsible for the needs of the men in getting the company captain in any area they may be in to provide guards at night, scouts, signallers, transport, suitable billets, boots and socks. Some small sum was given to each man to purchase cigarettes and to buy a few pints of porter at public houses in the particular district they may be in at the time. Battalion and some company officers at this inaugural launching of the nucleus of an army were not always available to take part in the fighting the column engaged in. They did take part from time to time but had to return to their own areas in the country districts to command and keep in training the various units comprising each battalion. Without this the column could not operate successfully. Volunteers were often called up from these companies to fight alongside the column men, as occasion demanded.

Tommy Leahy and myself returned to our area immediately after the formation of the column. At this time orders were received to raid the Post Office mails, and also to seize money from Post Offices. Any information of value that any letters contained written by policemen to relatives, or otherwise, sometimes gave an indication of the morale of that force.

Three of us one Friday evening raided the local Post Office and seized around £30. The postmaster was an uncle of one of us and had a reputation for tough lurid language and a hasty manner. This made him feared by old age pensioners and simple, rude unlettered individuals. We arrived at the Post Office with our faces covered with masks to guard against recognition, either by the postmaster or anybody else who might be there. It was laughable the effect our raid had on him. From being rude and domineering as he usually was, he became most obsequious to our demand that he hand over all monies in his charge. Our spokesman was his 18-year-old nephew, whom he titled "sir" in a frightened subservient manner. Still he did not lose his ability to swear luridly at an old age pensioner—Daniel Sullivan, who had his hand out to receive a ten shilling note from the postmaster. Daniel was so shocked at our appearance that he hesitated in the act of taking the note, only to see it vanish before his eyes into the hands of Jack our companion. We vanished quickly with the money up a laneway at the back and speculated at the postmaster's reaction to our visit, shaking with laughter as we did so.

During August, the homes of several I.R.A. men were searched by police and military, resulting in more and more men having to sleep away from home. In the various battalions at this time men worked on the farms by day, and slept in neighbouring houses in their own locality as well as attending drill parades at night, seeing after arms, signalling instructions, guard duty, dispatch work and transport facilities, etc.

This period heralded the first appearance in Abbeyfeale of the Black and Tans wearing that mixed uniform, thereafter getting their name from a celebrated hunt known by that appellation in East Limerick. They usually wore a pair of khaki pants, black jacket and peaked cap. The first detachment of this new force arrived in Abbeyfeale in early August, by the afternoon train.

Working in the meadow one fine evening I was surprised to see John Joe Leahy of Athea and Larry Ellen Harnett come in over the fence. They came to see me and impart some recent experience they had that morning at John Joe's home, where Larry was then staying, "on the run". He was making his way to join up with Sean Finn's column a few miles away near Ballyhahill. Sleeping on the one bed, in the early morning light, their slumber was rudely disturbed. Rushing into their room John Joe's father shouted, "Get out, the military are coming up the road from the village." Hastily snatching their clothes and guns they made their exit, through a window looking out into the farmyard, where just then the cows were being milked. They rushed into the shelter of a deep narrow glen overgrown with bushes and briars and extending up the steep hill beside the house. Here they dressed and made their way up, beneath its sheltering cover, until emerging on to the bare mountain of heather a good distance from the house. The military searched the house and surrounds, but did not venture up the hillside.

As a result of my talk with John Joe and Larry, I decided finally that it was not safe any longer to work at home. I said goodbye to my father, mother, sister Mary and my aunt for the time being. I secured the services of Danny Horgan, a young boy of fifteen, to stay in the house at night as company for my aunt. I collected my belongings and went for the first time "on the run". Securing billets for my two companions at Kelly's, who lived nearby, I got a bed for myself in a labourer's cottage a half-mile distant on the roadside. There I had my first contact with a truly venomous colony of fleas, who held a field day on my tender body when I retired to bed in a loft under the slates. As the night was sultry and humid it added to my discomfort. I said farewell to the fleas when I arose in the morning, consigning them to a hot region. From that night on and for many a day and night afterwards, there was a constant battle with vermin of another virulent kind, the deadly lice, the bane of our lives in prison and out of it.

On the day after my hopeless fight with the fleas, I contacted Tommy Leahy and our Adjutant Jack Aherne. Discussing
military matters amongst other things, we came up with the
bright idea that a week at the seaside in Ballybunion was just
what we wanted. So mounting our bicycles, we called at my
father's house to get, if possible, a few pounds to defray our
expenses for the trip. Sure enough he gave me a five pound
note and believed by so doing he was taking us away from
the danger of arrest. Continuing on our way with this windfall
to augment our low finances, we crossed the main road at
Templeglantine, continued on up Meenoline, bringing us out
on a road leading from Barna through Sugar Hill and
Knocknaboul into Athea village.

On the road near Sugar Hill, which was a steep upwards
climb, we wheeled our bicycles along. We met there a farmer
named Lar Curtin, who lived in a fine house overlooking
Barna, with the plains of Limerick spread below him stretching
to the Galtees. On recognising me, he enquired where we
were going. I told him we were "on the run" and making our
way to the West; that a bed someplace for the night was our
immediate concern. "Well!" said he, "Foley's of Sugar Hill is
the best place to make for as there you will be well looked
after." As he was about to leave he called me aside, and
pulling a five pound note from his pocket, he asked me to
accept it as an appreciation of our actions in the national
cause. To say that we were pleased would be an understate-
ment. In fact we were overwhelmed by such generosity,
making our trip to the seaside free from financial worry.

Bidding farewell to Lar Curtin, we thanked him sincerely,
mounted our bicycles and continued our journey to Foley's.
Here we stayed for the night with this hospitable family. Early
next morning we rode through Athea village, then to Moyvane
in Kerry. On our road west of Athea, we cycled by two
Crossley tenders on their way from their barrack in Tralee en
route to Newcastle West. We felt lucky that we escaped
without being halted and made to account for our movements
and to identify ourselves.

Arriving in Ballybunion, we secured accommodation in two houses, Jack Aherne and Tom Leahy in one, leaving me on my own to secure lodgings in another. During our stay of around a week at the seaside, we met others "on the run", from Dromcollogher and from North Cork. Whilst holidaying there my companions and myself enjoyed ourselves immensely, swimming, dancing and having a good time with some nice girls we had met. It was at one of these dances that I met my future wife. She was a nurse, then home on holiday from Gravesend Hospital, in London. After a week my two friends had about enough of the seaside, and left for home, a few days before I too departed. Bidding farewell reluctantly to my girl-friend and other boon companions, I departed on my bicycle for West Limerick.

On my arrival in early September I was astonished to learn that my two travelling companions, Jack Aherne and Tom Leahy, had seized the Post Office mails from Dinny Hunt the postman, who was bringing mail from Tournafulla to Newcastle West. They held up Dinny on the road outside the farmhouse of Mick H. Curtin, armed with two revolvers. Mrs. Mick Curtin, who was on the road at the time, witnessed the hold-up. She also saw a new arrival on the scene—Batt Wrenn, a farm worker and also a Volunteer who dismounted from his bicycle to join them. Allowing Dinny Hunt the time to cycle away and not report his hold-up for one hour, the boys, now joined by Batt Wrenn, opened a gate into a field adjoining the road in leisurely fashion and with some laughter and jokes sat down under a high hedge and proceeded to open the correspondence. The hold-up party had secured an endorsing lettered stamp and pad at the creamery and put "censored by the I.R.A." on each letter or document. The object of the whole business was to discover if there was a traitor in the locality, ready to barter information to the police for lucre or otherwise. Mrs. Curtin had in the meantime boiled the kettle, made some tea, cut some bread and brought out from her kitchen a picnic repast on a tray which made it look like a social gathering of friends under the autumn sunshine.

It was not to end as such, for scarcely had Mrs. Curtin arrived with the enjoyable repast and gone inside her farm gate into the field when the sound of a Crossley tender was heard, which was full of British troops. It stopped exactly where the hold-up had taken place, having just intercepted the postman minus his mailbag. Dinny was asked to point to the spot where the hold-up had taken place, and deemed it wise to do so. He assumed the boys would have in the meantime absconded, having heard the noise of the approaching lorry. Willie Curtin, creamery manager and his assistant Peter Curtin had a commanding view from their high second-story window of the ensuing encounter.

The Tans and soldiers stood on the slowly moving lorry and kept up a barrage of fire from the lorry on the three boys running close to the highly sheltered roadside fence. At a further adjoining fence running at right angles to above, Jack Aherne and Batt Wrenn ascended it, but Tommy Leahy retraced his steps under the shelter of the road fence, passing an open gateway on to the road, and was fired on. The Tans were unable to see adequately owing to the thorn hedge, and Mrs. Curtin's presence distracted them, so he arrived safely at the creamery. He was offered a bicycle to help him escape, but he declined as he coolly walked away down the fields. Jack and Batt were not so lucky as heavy fire was kept on them until Jack Aherne fell badly wounded, being shot through the neck. Both surrendered, as otherwise they would have been shot to pieces. Jack Aherne spent some weeks in a military hospital in Cork, and along with Batt Wrenn was sentenced to a long term of imprisonment in Ipswich Prison, England.

The reason for the quick arrival of the military and Tans so unexpectedly, was that Dinny Hunt, counter to the agreed delay of one hour, returned immediately to the Tournafulla Post Office a few miles from the hold-up to report to Larry Harnett, the postmaster there. This resulted in the speedy phone message to Newcastle head office, bringing quickly the arrival of the Tans and soldiers. A mistake was made by the hold-up party in not dismantling the telegraph wires by cutting them and also in not holding the postman during the censoring of the correspondence. The postmaster Larry Harnett swore luridly at the raiders' mistakes in the affair and was in a bad mood that evening, after Jack Aherne's mother verbally abused him for reporting the occurrence so quickly.

Late in September I spent a time with the Flying Column and was billeted with them in houses in Athea, Clounlehard, Kilcolman, Ballyhahill, Balliston and near Rathkeale. At the latter locality I spent a couple of nights at a farmer's place owned by a family by the name of Mulcahy. Whilst there I had the interesting experience of travelling over a forty acre field, where Dutch forces had encamped around the time of the Siege of Limerick. A large stone was erected in this field as a remembrance of those days, still vivid in Irish minds. It impressed me and reminded me of our continued struggle at that time, linking our struggle with that distant time, when Ireland had an army of her own, though siding with a cowardly monarch.

Returning to Athea, a discussion took place at a brigade council as to the feasibility of attacking the police and Tans at Abbeyfeale. The garrison in the barracks comprised a head constable, two sergeants and nineteen constables. We selected our ambush position at a crossroads known as Mountmahon on the outskirts of the town on the Tralee–Limerick main road. Our hope was that if we could get the police to congregate together at Mountmahon Cross, we could wipe out the patrol with a surprise attack, or failing this, compel their surrender and secure their arms. We kept our plans as secret as possible, so that no member of the population living in the town was aware. Knowing the locality well, I examined the position on the evening of the ambush, a short time before the attacking party arrived.

The ambush point was protected at the Newcastle side by a high stone wall enclosing the grounds of the Protestant Church and graveyard. Across the road facing the ambush position was a high fence on which grew a thick growth of whitethorn. At last all preparations were completed; armed men were placed on all roads leading to the town, telegraph lines were cut, scouts patrolled into the country to warn of any enemy approaching from the garrisons in Tralee or Newcastle West. Sections from each company of the Second Battalion moved into position.

About twenty-five men were placed inside the wall by the church. Commandant Finn took his place with around ten men, some armed with rifles, the rest with revolvers and shotguns, manning this wall. At his right men from the Abbeyfeale, Templeglantine and Tournafulla companies, armed in similar fashion took their places inside the fence of whitethorn. At the left of Finn's command post (as flank protection) four men were placed, myself included, armed with three rifles, one shotgun and revolvers. Jimmy Collins, Jackie O'Sullivan, Jim Roche and Tommy Leahy each commanded a section of these men, under Sean Finn's orders. Up the byroad, a few men armed with shotguns were placed behind the hedges, to prevent the police from retreating or using it to bring reinforcements.

The vanguard of the police patrol came up the road to Mountmahon Cross in extended order. Hearing strange sounds from the fence on their left, the police vanguard moved close to investigate the cause. One policeman peered in through the hedge and was shot dead as he looked into the face of one of the attackers. Right away a sustained fire was opened on the police and Tans, wounding five of them. After a short exchange of fire they retreated back towards the town leaving behind the dead man, Constable Mahony, but taking their wounded with them. During the engagement, two men jumped out on the road and lying down behind a large heap of stones fired down the road on the police until they disappeared into the shelter of their barracks. Our force suffered no casualties in this conflict. That night the column retreated safely to Athea, six miles away.

Early in October the Flying Column left Athea district and moved to Clounleharde and Grouse Lodge, where some of the boys, myself included, stayed at O'Donovan's, a favourite house for all. Sean Finn, O/C, stayed for a few days. Whilst there Sean received information from Mick Murphy, Captain of Pallaskenry Company, that it was possible to attack a patrol of police in that village. Arrangements were made to move our billets at O'Donovan's and from the houses in its vicinity. We left one evening and marched near Rathkeale, at a place called Newbridge, on the Foynes road between both towns. I, with Finn and others, were given shelter in houses in that locality. The house I stayed in belonged to a family of O'Donnell's who owned a fine house and farm. Mrs. O'Donnell was anxious to get all the news about my native place, Tournafulla, as she herself came from there. So ensued a pleasant conversation until we retired for the night. On this march we did not get any protection from the local Volunteers as our plans and destination were kept a close secret. As a result we had to post our own armed guards on outposts, each having to do four hours in rotation on this duty.

On leaving O'Donnell's we got a scout to bring us across country the following night, bringing us nearer the Shannon and our objective. We traversed over fields, hedges, and along pathways behind double ditches, protected by impenetrable hedges made weird and gloomy as it was difficult to see more than a few feet. They made a safe refuge and protection even in daylight. They often extended for miles and are a feature of the landscape in Co. Limerick. Their shelter was extensively used by the flying columns in moving from place to place and helped to save them from hostile enemy operations in their vicinity.

Finally we arrived near the main Limerick-to-Foynes road. We secured billets in some houses to the east of Askeaton, in from the road. Our column of about 20 men was armed with rifles, shotguns, revolvers and grenades. Our beds were laid on the floor of the parlour, with mattresses and anything handy to make up a huge bed. This was the arrangement in the house in which I was billeted with Sean Finn and about 12 comrades. We lay down, side by side, without undressing— our weapons near us—to seek an uneasy sleep. Each in turn had to do guard duty in the yard facing the road. Many a rough joke was made between us at our situation. Larry Ellen Harnett, a great joker, predicted that it was but a preparation for our future status as convicts. "Our Republic", said Larry, "is but a myth and a dream. I can see us all in a convict ship. It stares us in the face, God help us!" This, and other tough jests we were well used to in a company where imprisonment and worse was always near at hand.

When my time to do duty came it was about dawn of day. Suddenly I heard in the distance the noise of a motor vehicle, increasing in volume as it drew nearer. I stood momentarily immobile as two Crossley tenders, filled with police, Auxiliaries and Tans, passed along clearly visible to me in the increasing light. I quickly made for the doorway into the parlour where I alerted my companions to our danger. We immediately came outside and routed out the others in the neighbouring house. We had scarcely taken our places behind a fence when more lorries appeared, their occupants firing their rifles indiscriminately in every direction. We moved from our position undiscovered, with rifle bullets whining over our heads. Then we withdrew in the semi-light of the morning further away from the road into fields protected by high hedges. Establishing our position in the mind of our scout, we directed him to make contact with Mick Murphy, Captain of Pallaskenry Coy. This he did, knowing where he probably could be found. Mick Murphy was then "on the run", and usually slept away from home. He kept to his own locality and carried out his duties there, assisted by the Neville brothers, prominent in the I.R.A., and others. When he arose that morning information was brought to him that a large force of military, Auxiliaries and Tans had thrown a cordon around the country in the vicinity of Pallaskenry and were engaged in the encirclement of the district. When he was told where we were he hurried to meet us. After consultation it was agreed that for the present we should withdraw from the district.

We withdrew in the direction of Rathkeale, keeping to the fields and only traversing stretches of byroads when necessary. After walking several miles we arrived near the mansion of a country gentleman. This man was known to one of our boys, Johnny Glinny, whose sister was housekeeper to him. On the strength of Johnny's tenuous acquaintance with the owner, we decided we could not travel another step without sustenance. We were exhausted, and though we knew our presence would not be welcome to the owner, we had no other option. Knocking at the door of this imposing edifice, we were confronted by the owner, who reluctantly admitted us. He was truly frightened when he saw our armed men invade his home, settle down on comfortable chairs and couches in his beautiful sitting room. Soon we had whiskey and porter glasses in our hands and the bottles on the sideboard to regale ourselves with. Johnny's sister prepared a generous meal for us and I can tell you we made short work of it. This gentleman farmer was on tenter-hooks whilst we lingered, consuming his drink and food and probably consigning us to a warm climate.

Looking out of his large dining room windows we had a splendid view of Rathkeale town, perched on an eminence of the rolling countryside. There, distinctly visible, was the police barracks, set apart in isolation on a little hillock. The town and barracks were uncomfortably close to our present refuge for any lingering there by us. Despite the drowsy feeling creeping over us we thanked our host and housekeeper and departed for the western hills, reaching them late at night.

In November we lost some officers captured in raids by military and police. Battalion Adjutant Danny Curtin, Sonny Quaid (Capt. Athea Coy.), and Jim Roche (Capt. Templeglantine Coy.), and others were interned in Ballykinlar and in Spike Island. On the night Danny Curtin's home was raided Tommy Leahy was at Mrs. Kelly's, a few hundred yards away, staying the night. Hearing the rumble of lorries in the distance, and seeing the reflection of their lights on the horizon as they approached from Newcastle West, he ran quickly towards Danny's house. He just reached a fence a short distance from Curtin's farmhouse, intending to warn Danny of the military in the immediate vicinity, but they beat him to it and knocked thunderously at the door demanding admittance. Danny was roughly routed out of bed, and got only a short time to dress as they ransacked the house.

Someone must have informed the police as to Danny's importance in the I.R.A. He was our second Battalion Adjutant, appointed after Jack Aherne was wounded and captured six weeks previously. Once more, a vacancy for this position led to the appointment of Aeneas Sheahan, who unfortunately died a few months afterwards. These arrests continued from time to time all over West Limerick, as elsewhere, and necessitated filling of vacant ranks.

My home in Killaculleen was raided at dawn of day by a strong force of Tans and Auxiliaries. They terrorised my Aunt Mary and Danny Horgan, the young boy who had just left school. They demanded to know where I was and poor Danny was subjected to terrorist methods, but he courageously refused to disclose my whereabouts. It was only a few days previously that I had paid a visit home to see how things were going on. On that visit I was accompanied by some boys of the column. Paddy Naughton, one of them, was a native of Limerick City, who earlier in the year had attacked two R.I.C. men in the Railway Hotel in that city. He entered the hotel in daylight, opened fire on the police with a Webley revolver, mortally wounding one and slightly wounding the other. As a result he had to flee the city as the injured policemen recognised him. He was in the West Limerick Flying Column with a price on his head and instant execution if captured. Paddy made a solemn vow that he'd never surrender but fight it out to death if confronted with this dire possibility. He was most peculiar about his diet, always carried a loaf of home-baked brown bread in his haversack. He never ate meat of any sort but lived on this bread with milk, butter, eggs and tea. He was as active as any of the others, could endure cold, heat, hardship and long marches day and night. He was fairly tall, of angular build, wide hips, pointed chin and thin pointed nose. When we were billeted in some farmhouse at night Paddy was in demand as a singer of note, to entertain us before sleeping. He had a good tenor voice and his rendering of the patriotic ballads stirred our hearts.

Paddy's finger was never far away from the trigger of the weapon in his hands. One had to be careful approaching the house he was billeted in, for if his challenge went unanswered it was at once followed by a rifle shot from his ever-ready gun. Referring to the evening when Paddy and the others accompanied me to see my aunt, a near fatal accident took place. We were all standing and chatting on the porch of our house. A hall door led into this porch, then from there a doorway led into the kitchen and another into the parlour. Built into the wall of this porch was a small window through which could be seen anyone sitting beside the open kitchen fire. My aunt was sitting in a sugan chair with her back to the wall, facing this little window. As we chatted together and joked about things relevant to our hunted existence our peace was suddenly shattered by a loud, deafening explosion. In amazement we saw the rifle in Paddy Naughton's hands pointed toward the little window I have mentioned. It appeared he just pulled the trigger unconsciously, unaware that the cut-off was not in place. Immediately we rushed into the kitchen to see my aunt in a state of collapse and right beside where she was sitting was a big slice of wall plaster lying on the ground. We could not find the bullet as it probably penetrated far into the wall between the stones; in old houses these walls were often two feet wide. It was a truly frightening experience for anyone to undergo, much less a woman. We hadn't even a drop of spirits in the house to restore her shattered nerves. I usually had to suffer in silence the recriminations that came my way as a result of this and other episodes at that time.

During November 1920 the organisation of the I.R.A. was being perfected in many ways all over the country. The engineer's section in all company areas was organised to make mines, bombs, to learn how to demolish bridges, and to block roads by a system of trenches. These latter were made in sections of a road difficult to by-pass without adequate planks to span the trenched roads. They were placed in hollow sections impossible to see; no trace was visible to the driver of a fast-driven vehicle. Many such cars were wrecked as a result and injuries often inflicted on driver and occupants. These trenches were specially designed; three cuttings were made, none fully across the road, in a zigzag fashion. On bog roads or solid surfaces it was important that the land inside the trenched road could not be used by opening gaps at either side to facilitate by-passing the cuttings. All these tactics delayed enemy round-ups and provided ample time for columns and wanted men to retire to safer country. The signallers, now posted regularly round the clock, were able to give timely notice of the approaching military and police. In the following months many a man living near these trenches was now also "on the run" pro tem, as on hearing the rumble of the Crossley tenders he sought safety in the fields until the danger had passed.

Old and young, if caught by the enemy, were pressed into service to fill up these cuttings. The farmers carting milk to the creameries and people attending fairs and markets, were sometimes stopped and compelled to fill in these trenches, equipped with inadequate implements. Some old people, looking simple but highly intelligent, put on an act for the benefit of the soldiers as to their inability to do such strenuous labour. Tom Collins, an old age pensioner, on being stopped on the road from the creamery by the military, started to wheeze and cough as copious tears coursed down his cheeks. He looked so distressed and hoarse that a couple of soldiers evinced sympathy for him, conveyed him from the danger zone and repeatedly asked him "Will you be alright father? Go to bed father, be sure you treat your cold when you reach home."

The column spent some time in the parish of Glin, billeted in houses overlooking the lordly Shannon. I often looked out over the river where two gunboats were lying at anchor with the flag of England flying from their mastheads. Little did they know that their mortal enemies on the hills viewed their armed might with little concern or spent any sleepless nights on their account. While in that locality we paid nightly calls to Glin village to buy cigarettes or a few drinks at John Conway's hotel, or other licensed premises. Admirers of ours there very often treated us to drinks generously; often resulting in hilarious sessions being held in the hotel or public houses.

Towards the close of 1920 a party of Black and Tans were ambushed by the column at a place called Barrygone, between Foynes and Askeaton. At regular intervals they travelled by train from Foynes to Limerick. Our officers held a meeting to decide the most advantageous point to attack and we agreed on Barrygone. The time they usually travelled on the train was noted and the day each week that this took place.

Eighteen men were selected under the command of Sean Finn, Garrett McAuliffe and Michael Colbert, to occupy the selected position—a high rocky limestone escarpment over-looking a deep cutting through which the train passed. One Volunteer, Con Boyle, took his place on the tracks and held up a red flag to halt the oncoming train. The cutting was occupied by nine men on either side sheltering behind the rocky boulders around which they had to fire downwards at the Black and Tans who were seated in compartments of the train which consisted of two carriages, engine and guards van. The Tans for safety were scattered throughout the carriages and their party comprised around twelve men, two together in the same compartment guarding each side against attack.

A Volunteer named Liston travelled on the train from Foynes, whose duty it was to wave his cap to notify the ambush party as to the number of police as it approached the ambush position. Con Boyle, whose duty it was to halt the train had a dangerous assignment as he took his place on the line, waving his flag and stopping the train. Having done so he scrambled up the steep rocky side of the cutting to rejoin his comrades. Immediately the train stopped and heads were seen looking out the windows to ascertain the cause. At once a fusillade of rifle and shotgun bullets rang out as fire was opened on the Tans, visible inside. Unfortunately, civilians were travel-ling in the train and they had miraculous escapes. Lying on the floor, they tried to find refuge there from the stream of bullets and shotgun pellets. Up on the rock embankments chips off the stone were flying dangerously around, being sliced into lethal weapons by the bullets fired by the Tans. The firing continued for a time and it was observed that some of the police were wounded. A brave Black and Tan was seen to jump out of the train, crawl along the cutting to the engine where he jumped inside and threatened the driver with his gun, compelling him to start his engine and draw away from the zone of battle. So ended a furious fight, whilst it lasted, causing great disappointment to our men at the outcome.

Our force suffered no casualties and though disheartened by the outcome the experience provided useful knowledge for the future. Our greatest loss was to lose ammunition, always in short supply, and failure to capture any weapons from the enemy—which our guerilla force much depended on to arm extra men. The column, after this train attack, moved westwards into the friendly hills and was billeted amongst the hospitable people who inhabited them.

In December we moved into the eastern district of Abbeyfeale, at Meenahela, Kileenagh and Ballycommane. With the friendly Barrett family and three nice girls to look after us we spent some pleasant days there. Dances and songs were a must at night. The home of Biddy Forde where I was staying with Con Cregan, Jack Leahy and Michael Colbert was a hospitable place. Biddy, a handsome young girl, made the time feel short. Being a good conversationalist and singer she entertained us nightly, assisted in her songs by some of our own outlawed Raparees, notably Paddy Naughton and Patie O'Neill.

After some days in the area of Abbeyfeale the column moved away to Templeglantine and then to Sugar Hill. I did not go with them but attended company parades and council meetings at battalion and company level. Since our holiday in Ballybunion I kept up a correspondence with the nurse I had met there and I proposed marriage as a suitable end to our romance. It was a foolish proposal under the circumstances of my being a wanted man, in constant danger nearly all the time. The brave girl agreed to my proposition and of course was as foolish as myself. So it was arranged, accompanied by Jack Leahy, also "on the run", as groomsman. We arrived at the home of John Walsh, father of my promised bride, Julia Walsh, in the Parish of Ballydonohue, sister Parish of Ballybunion. It was a dark evening in December 1920 when we left Abbeyfeale region, travelling by pony and trap, driven by Jimmy Sullivan. On our way we met Paddy Walsh at Gunsboro, also a wanted man and I.R.A. Captain. He and others had, a short time previously, attacked a patrol of about four police at a place called Bedford. In the exchange of shots Sergeant McKenna was killed and a few others wounded before they surrendered and gave up their arms. Paddy Walsh was a first cousin of my future wife, shortly to be murdered by the Tans.

On a dark morning, 22 December, 1920, we got out of our beds in the gloom and mist creeping down from Knockanore Hill and made our way over the fields to the church. My bride was accompanied by her sister Bridgie and her brother Mick. Jack Leahy and myself walked together but apart from the others; to keep an old custom this was necessary. It was thought too, that it was not the proper thing that I should have slept in the bride's home before being married but circumstances prevented me from doing otherwise. As we came near the church we were alarmed at seeing about six armed men dash out from the sacristy and disappear in the semi-darkness of this December morning. Some weeks later I met one of the I.R.A. who had left so hurriedly that morning, Dan Sullivan. He told me that they were ready to open fire on us as they thought our party to be members of the Black and Tans on an early morning raid. Around that period searches in churches were becoming commonplace. So ended my romantic love affair if it can be designated as such. It led in the coming months to my close association with some members of the No. 1 Kerry Brigade I.R.A., who subsequently were killed in action and others murdered by Auxiliaries and Tans.

My friend Jack Leahy and myself spent the Christmas season in Kerry. We slept in neighbouring houses at night and spent our days at Walsh's. There we had the unnerving experience of seeing Crossley tenders filled with Auxiliaries and Tans pass by on the Listowel–Ballybunion Road, close to the house. Jack felt in real danger and I myself felt the same. The police had a habit of firing shots at houses and people working in the fields. About a half mile away, an old farmer, going about his daily avocation, was shot dead in a field near to his home.

About a week after Christmas Jack Leahy decided he had about enough of North Kerry and was fed up, so Paddy Walsh of Gunsboro guided him as far as Moyvane and from there he travelled alone through Athea and Templeglantine until he reached his native district. I stayed on in Kerry for another week or so and slept in the home of Ned Purtell for a few nights. Old Ned's son, Mick, was an officer in the local I.R.A. company and an uncle of John B. Keane, the playwright.

I changed my nightly abode frequently and at the home of the Dowlings in Gunsboro shared a bed with Tomas O'Donoghue, T.D. for Kerry at that time. Tomas was a wanted man, a native of South Kerry, and a fluent Irish speaker. He had endured cruel treatment in England during the Great War because as a conscientious objector to military service he refused to serve in the army. As a result he spent some years in prison in England subjected to terrible indignities. For several days he was compelled to stand in his cell in water a couple of feet deep. His prison ration of food was curtailed; it consisted of the bare minimum. His fortitude and will alone sustained him in his lonely cell and faith in his Maker. The result of such treatment brought on severe rheumatism; a complaint he had constantly to bear. This disease was an added hardship to him whilst "on the run". He regularly tramped the countryside with the North Kerry Column and took part in their engagements.

In February 1921, British military forces were stationed in Rathkeale and Newcastle West. They moved into the country in armoured cars and Crossley tenders, committing outrages, such as beating and murdering civilians, burning houses and public buildings. By these tactics they created a difficult situation for our small column. As the danger was real it was decided at a brigade council to enlist the aid of the East Limerick Flying Column. Plans were submitted to Donncadh O'Hannigan, Column Commander, Sean Wall, Brigade O/C, and other officers for an attack on the military forces regularly moving between Newcastle West to Abbeyfeale, or, on the forces patrolling between Foynes and Newcastle West. Athea was fixed as the rendezvous for both flying columns to meet. In mid-March the East Limerick men under O'Hannigan marched from the Tipperary border, across the plains of Limerick in two night marches. They comprised some fifty well-armed men, and at the rear was a horse-drawn cart with mines and explosives. On arrival at Athea the men were billeted in selected farmhouses while a favourable opportunity was awaited to carry out an organised attack on the enemy.

Next morning being Sunday, all the men went to confession in order to receive Holy Communion during Mass in Athea Church. During the day information was received that there was extraordinary activity by the Crown Forces in Newcastle West. On receipt of this news the two columns now united under O'Hannigan and Finn moved to the high hills between Athea and Ballyhahill where they spent the night, a cold, bitter one, with driving sleet and rain. On this high ground, with little shelter, they awaited the morning prepared to fight it out with the enemy. During the night the rumble of lorries was heard and their lights visible in the distance as they patrolled the roads sweeping the countryside with searchlights. They failed to find our men and withdrew temporarily. On Monday night our men withdrew to the next district, Ballyhahill, about five miles north near the Shannon. The Column now numbered nearly seventy-five men and occupied houses extending over a wide area in a circle enclosing the village of Ballyhahill.

The military, in their withdrawal from the Athea region, left behind them an armoured car, temporarily out of action, and a gun-crew to protect it. A section of our boys seeing this armoured car, alone and isolated on a bare stretch of bog road, advanced in open formation down the barren hillside in an effort to capture it. It would be suicidal to attempt it as the machine gun in its revolving turret covered all approaches to it. A consultation was held and the decision reached that in open daylight it would be impossible to capture it and that only in the darkness of night could it possibly succeed. That road would soon be a real danger zone as a quick rescue of the armoured car was imminent, and so it was. Our men had only withdrawn over the brow of the hill when the noise of reinforcements was heard as the Crossley tenders rumbled in the distance and swiftly approached the stranded armoured car.

During the following day the men rested from the hardships of the previous night. In the afternoon three of the East Limerick men who were billeted on the southeast of the village went to a crossroads house to get their shoes mended. They were not long there when scouts reported the rapid advance of enemy forces in Crossley tenders. Having left their rifles in their billet the men rushed out and were fired on by the military as they ran to get their rifles. Back at their billet the three I.R.A. men were immediately engaged by over forty of the enemy who besieged them. Staying near them in a large farmhouse were the Column Commander O'Hannigan, Sean Finn, O/C, Jim Colbert, Quartermaster, West Limerick Brigade, and Volunteer Seamus Finn. The three besieged men, on signals given on a whistle by their leader O'Hannigan, fought their way out of the house to rejoin their comrades. These three men were Volunteers Quane, Howard, and Walsh. The seven men engaged in a running battle over the fields and forts which lasted about an hour. During the battle some of the soldiers fell before the rifles of the I.R.A. men and some were mortally wounded. In the fighting young Quane, shot through the neck, was badly wounded. He begged his comrades to leave him as he would only be an impediment to them. This they refused to do and brought him with them. Called on repeatedly to surrender, this they never contemplated. They continued the fight in the hope that the men of the column, hearing the gunfire, would come to their assistance, but this did not happen. The fight continued for about two hours and as the men ran across a field to take up a stand behind a high fence, Sean Finn was seen to fall mortally wounded; his rifle whirled in the air. Behind this fence they turned their guns on the enemy and as one Tan more daring than the rest moved towards Sean Finn's body, Volunteer Howard calmly shot him down. At this stage the party, now six, one of them badly wounded, were running low in ammunition. Then was enacted one of the bravest deeds seen in any encounter at that time. O'Hannigan, realising the seriousness of the loss of Sean Finn's rifle and ammunition, and further by the news that Seamus Finn was now without any ammunition, came to a desperate decision. He asked for a Volunteer to go out into the bullet-scarred field to recover the rifle and ammunition of their dead comrade. Young Finn at once dashed out to the body, lying midway in the field between them and the enemy. Covered by the fire of his comrades, as enemy bullets cut the field around him, he succeeded in securing both gun and ammunition and ran swiftly back to his comrades.

The fight went on as the I.R.A. men doubled back, running behind hedges in zigzag fashion as they confronted the Crown Forces now on one front, then dashing away over a fence to open fire from a right angle position on any Tans crossing into the field just evacuated. Again changing direction, they took shelter in a rath at the other side of the field. Some three and a half hours had now passed with some easing off by the military and Tans, but some Black and Tans were now seen approaching cautiously towards their screen of thorn bushes that grew on the perimeter of their refuge. Just then happened one of those unpredictable occurrences. Up from the Shannon river crept swiftly a welcome fog to blot out the landscape. It gave pause to the enemy advance, as they, not being familiar with the district, now called a halt to their advance. They gradually withdrew to their lorries, taking Finn's body and their own dead and wounded with them, and cleared out to return to their barracks.

On the field of battle O'Hannigan promoted Seamus Finn to 1st Lieutenant, and later this appointment was confirmed by

G.H.Q. After a time the fog lifted and Jim Colbert saw a local farmer inspecting the scene of the fight. Cautiously he was called to where they sheltered, informing them of the departure of the enemy. They departed supporting Quane, who had by now lost a lot of blood. Later that night he was taken to a friendly house near Glin where Dr. Enright of Listowel examined and dressed his wounds.

Making contact with J. T. O'Connor, O/C 5th Battalion, sent to discover their whereabouts, they returned cautiously, still hearing enemy whistles in the distance and arrived back with the main body of men assembled in positions commanding the approaches to Ballyhahill. They remained there until 3 a.m. the following morning, then retreated westwards to Kilbaha, Co. Kerry. Now that the element of a surprise attack was out of the question, with overwhelming Crown Forces combing this West Limerick area, it was decided to evacuate the district for the time being. So began for the combined columns another successful march back to Tipperary border. They reached their destination in about two nights or more, marching by way of Kilcolman, Pallaskenry and Grannagh, using the roads all the time until reaching the friendly Galtees. Back in the East they were joined by a column of men under Commdt. "Sean Forde" and Commdt. Sean Carroll of the Mid-Limerick Brigade, making a total of nearly ninety men. This combined force saw continuous fighting for six weeks and participated in the fighting at Lackelly and Emly. One East Limerick and three Mid-Limerick men were killed in the battles and encounters that took place throughout April 1921. Tom Howard, who fought so bravely at Ballyhahill, was mortally wounded in one of these battles, as was Danny Murphy of Abbeyfeale.

At the end of this period the West Limerick men were recalled and on their march back rested in the vicinity of Granagh. There a court martial was held and a confirmed spy captured a short time before was sentenced to death. A party of Fourth Battalion West Limerick men in command of Lieut. Michael O'Shea were taking this spy to the place of execution when, as they marched along in the darkness of night, they were challenged to halt. They replied that they were I.R.A., thinking that their challengers were their comrades. Disillusion came quickly as they were greeted by a fusillade of rifle shots from a patrol of military from the nearby camp at Ballyvonare. This resulted in mortally wounding Second Lieut. Michael O'Shea and dangerously wounding Volunteer Patrick Benson. In the ensuring confusion the spy escaped and sought refuge with the military patrol into whose ranks he crawled for safety. Michael O'Shea did not die at once but did so shortly afterwards in the custody of the enemy, where also Patrick Benson found himself, but he eventually recovered from his wounds.

Brigade Vice Commdt. Garrett McAuliffe and the commdts. of the five battalions, myself included, did not accompany our men to East Limerick. Those who went were placed under the command of Michael Colbert as their leader. Headquarters in Dublin sent us a staff officer as organiser to train active service units and plan future engagements. He had the fictitious name of "Capt. Hand". I took him on an inspection of all our companies in the Second Battalion. During one of these training exercises at an old farmhouse (abandoned), known as the cover because of the dense shrubbery surrounding it, "Capt. Hand" demonstrated the usefulness of bayonet fighting. He went through all the intricacies of such method of fighting with a rifle and bayonet. The boys and myself were highly amused at such a display. Discussing it afterwards we agreed that if we could have sufficient rifles we would not need the bayonets.

CHAPTER V.

TRUCE AND TREATY, 1921.

In April a brigade council was held somewhere near Foynes. Its object was to elect a commanding officer for the brigade, now necessary, as this position was vacant since March when Sean Finn was killed in action. On the instructions of G.H.Q., "Capt. T. Hand" was ordered to convene the council and make a recommendation to it as to who should be selected as Brigade O/C. The commdts. of the five battalions attended and had no option but to agree. So Garrett McAuliffe, Vice Commdt., was appointed without dissent. His record was a good one and he had good experience as a fighter, having taken part as a Volunteer in the G.P.O. during Easter Week, fought at Kilmallock and elsewhere. Accompanied by 3rd Battalion officers Con. Foley and Ben Sullivan of Dromcollogher, I travelled to the council. Armed with three rifles, Con and Ben came westwards from Drom to meet me, and we crossed the country over hills and dales until reaching the home of Bob Cullhane, situated on high ground overlooking the Shannon and Glin village. There we slept for the night and enjoyed all the jokes passed around between Ben, who was always ready for fun with a fund of stories, and some nice girls we met there, who kept us entertained. Continuing from there we made our way through Ballyhahill and Clounlehard, finally emerging from the hills at Glensharald and so onwards to our destination. Ben and Con had, with others, tramped all the long miles from Dromcollogher to Clounbannon on the Kerry border in Ballydesmond known also as Sliebe Luachra but a short while before this. Their aim was to take part in the attack planned by North Cork Flying Column Commdt. Sean Moylan. This fight lasted some hours during which General Cummins, commanding the enemy force, was killed. It was an inconclusive conflict and eventually the Cork and Kerry I.R.A. withdrew under fire from the Auxiliaries and Black and Tans who occupied inaccessible vantage points. They had abandoned their transport at the start of the fight and sought cover, placing themselves so that they were prepared with abundant ammunition to hold out all day. Against them the I.R.A., to whom every shot counted; this meant a loss that could not be permitted and also the danger from enemy reinforcements.

In our brigade we had some demobbed soldiers who had a few years previously fought in the Great War. The experiences gained by them then was of great value to us and was availed of by us wholeheartedly. Pat Fitzgerald, born in New Zealand of Irish parents, was a character in himself. His accent intrigued us and caused fun amongst us as well as a few digs occasionally at the cockney in our ranks. He assumed the role of father confessor and advisor to the O/C, but we remained sceptical of the role he assumed.

Hell was created for us by the constant company of lice who fattened on us and multiplied rapidly on our shirts and in the bedclothes where we slept, thereby creating another hell in every house we stayed in. All sorts of devices were tried to clean our shirts and bed sheets, in every seam of these garments this vermin sought shelter and the women had a tough task with red hot iron to eradicate them in a losing battle. We too, took a hand at this business ourselves by trying to maintain a semblance of cleanliness, but it was hopeless. Bed bugs were also terrible company at night as I discovered to my cost at a small farmer's house, built in the middle of cut-away bogland. There in ceaseless activity these vermin pursued me through the night as I prayed for the dawn. Virulent itch this spring added to our torments as it spread rapidly amongst our boys. It was designated "The Republican Itch" and none escaped its ravages.

Dirty conditions, dirty beds, unkempt clothing, all contributed to our unenviable misery. Unavoidable, considering the conflict we were engaged in—sleeping in hay barns, lying beside fences, wading across streams, rarely changing shirts or socks. No baths were available; primitive washing at all times did not help. Many a housewife with clean bed linen must have consigned us to perdition as on departing we left her a legacy and reminder of our stay. That embarrassed some of us, at least. True to say some of the I.R.A. never gave it a thought, or even felt discomfort by the vermins' viciousness. I believe some had skins like leather, impervious to attack. Conditions were so bad in a house where two of the boys and myself slept one night that we decided to place the quilt on the bed, under us, cover ourselves with our trench coats and keep our clothes on, resting uneasily until morning. That was a bad night for us and we had many such ordeals frequently.

During this spring my father's home was surrounded and searched by a party of Tans in the early hours one morning. They enquired as to my whereabouts and behaved in a very rough manner to my parents and sisters. This was their usual method all over Ireland and civilians were subjected to abuse and unprintable language used as the Tans beat them up to try to bolster their very shaken morale. Our invisible army gave them the creeps in their assailable motor transport on many an encounter. Their seeming invincibility was of no avail against the shotguns at close quarters.

On coming home to get a change of shirt and socks from my mother one Saturday evening, I was persuaded to stay for the night. My companion on many adventures, Jack Leahy, was billeted a few hundred yards to the west, in the farmhouse of the Murphys. Both houses were on the road leading eastwards to the church. This road joined the Limerick to Tralee highway, frequently patrolled by strong police and military forces. On arising Sunday morning I got ready to attend early morning Mass but my mother persuaded me to stay away as raids were by now becoming frequent on churches. I was lucky that I took her advice. As I knelt down to say my prayers,

suddenly I was disturbed by the sound of gunfire coming from
the direction of Murphys. It continued for about ten minutes
and the noise made by the military lorries coming up a steep
hill beside the farmhouse was unnerving. The next thing I
remember was that they were on the road outside our house.
I ran quickly out of the house, into the yard, screened from
view by a thorn hedge, then ran through the cowshed into a
field at the rear. Now, to my horror, this field was not protected
by any hedge and was beside the road travelled by police and
military. As I jumped into this field I saw out of the corner of
my eye the tailend of a Crossley tender passing into the shelter
of the hedge that grew on the roadside in front of the house
and haggard. Immediately following the Crossley was a private
car about twenty yards behind; I could see its occupants
distinctly as its side was open with a canvas hood. Having an
unrestricted view from the field I entered I hesitated, then
jumped back again. It surprised me that I was not observed;
the reason was that this military party was on its way to surround the parish church and search the congregation. Hence
their hurry before any wanted man was made aware of their
approach and escape.

My comrade, Jack Leahy, was surprised and alarmed on
hearing the noise of the lorries as they drove up the hill.
Escaping out a back window of the house he ran across a
sloping field in full view of the enemy driving up this hill.
Immediately fire was opened on him; some of the Auxiliaries
jumped out of the Crossleys and ran after him, pumping lead
at him as he ran. After a few minutes he crossed over a big
ditch and bank into another bare field. This gave him a few
minutes out of sight of his enemies to cross it like a greyhound
and dive into a deep ravine with steep cut sides covered with
briars, furze bushes, and high ferns. He ran down to the
stream until reaching a little bridge spanning the road about
two hundred yards distant. Under the eye of this small stone
bridge he sought refuge and found the entrance on either side
covered with a luxuriant growth of ivy, ferns and bushes,
making a precious screen against discovery.

He would, undoubtedly, have been discovered if the search for him had been protracted. In fact he could see one Tan staring through the foliage and expected to be discovered any moment. This would certainly have happened, but a whistle was then blown by an officer calling off the chase. He never stirred until a woman, living beside the bridge, seeing the military and police withdraw, cautiously approached to tell him that they were gone.

Abandoning their search for Jack Leahy they drove quickly in their Crossley tenders to surround the church. On arrival, as the 9 o'clock Mass was being said by Father Michael Ryan, they mounted a number of machine guns on the walls surrounding the grounds. Previously, during the night, they had taken possession of an abandoned farmhouse (owned by John Scanlon) about a couple of hundred yards from the church. There they placed a decoy of about nine Black and Tans dressed just like the I.R.A., in breeches, yellow leggings, trench coats, and caps. All were fully armed with revolvers and service rifles. For any fleeing I.R.A. men seeing them it would seem a God-send to have such succour close at hand. Luckily enough there were no boys "on the run" at mass that morning—I myself, as related, stayed at home at my mother's request.

When a son of John Scanlon, Mossie, went to his father's old farmhouse to fodder cattle housed there, he was arrested and kept for a considerable time. Another parishioner, Denis O'Sullivan, called "Johnston", a very talkative individual, generally rode on horseback to Mass. On entering the house to stable his horse he was astonished to see the place filled with armed men. As they laid hands on him to prevent him leaving he got angry, believing them to be I.R.A. men. He abused them and accused them of being better employed in ambushing the Tans. Too late he discovered his mistake as he heard them speaking with English accents. They roughly manhandled him, striking him with their rifle butts. Later he and Mossie Scanlon were released, but not until the search of the people, men and women, attending Mass was over.

Mass was on when the military, led by a captain in the Warwicks from Newcastle West, marched up the centre aisle as Father Ryan was celebrating Mass. The people (some in a panic), on seeing the soldiers enter, fled inside the altar rails around the priest. Cooly turning to the officer, Father Ryan remonstrated at the behaviour of himself and his hirelings, requesting that they leave during divine service. After some delay the military officer complied and withdrew outside where they placed themselves around both doorways. On leaving the church at the end of Mass the people were searched by Tans and women searchers. Father Ryan by his coolness, and calm exhortations to his flock, brought order into a very dangerous situation.

During his ministry in our parish, Father Ryan endeared himself to young and old and in his work as president of the Sinn Féin court was scrupulous in striving for justice in court decisions. During his long life he had fond memories of his stay amongst us and work performed for our moral, spiritual and material benefit.

In this raid on our church only one I.R.A. man, Volunteer Dinny Wrenn, was arrested. He was roughly handled and thrown into the body of one of the lorries where he was hand-cuffed and chained to an iron bar. Taken to Newcastle military establishment at the castle he was then brought out into a courtyard at the back and put standing by the side of an open grave. A firing party of military took up position facing him, then warned by an officer of what his fate would be (instant death) if he did not answer truthfully as to the whereabouts of Tommy Leahy, myself, and others prominent in the district. Dinny Wrenn was one of the most courageous boys in the I.R.A. and this was a well-known fact to his comrades. Silently and doggedly he resisted all threats and physical abuse. Early next morning he was released and brought home by the military.

One night in April the Black and Tans came to Meenahela, a townland near Tournafulla, and ransacked the creamery. They stole butter, cream, and any cash that was there. I was staying at Barretts, a few hundred yards away. Jim Barrett and myself moved near and as we took shelter behind a hedge, had a good view of their activities. The lights from their cars illuminated the scene, to disclose to us their whereabouts as they busily loaded boxes of butter on to one of their lorries. They did not linger long but moved off towards Abbeyfeale.

Our Vice-Commdt. Jimmy Collins, with some other officers and myself, decided to ambush them near the town of Abbeyfeale and planned as to the best way to do so. Having got some members of the column to carry out this attack, assisted by local I.R.A. men, we assembled at a place called Kileenagh, a few miles distant from the town, and waited there for the day arranged. We intended to wait for them in houses in the town itself. Each morning their usual procedure was to patrol the streets in open formation. The number engaged in this exercise was usually about ten men. These patrols were never seen in the town except in the early hours of the summer mornings before the townspeople arose.

It did not come off because during the appointed night a large force of military, about one hundred men, swooped on the town around dawn. They had marched from Newcastle West through Ardagh, Carrickerry, and Athea, to enter the town and take over the place. There was no chance to carry out our intended attack. Our intelligence noted their strength and reported their activities to us during the morning. We were disappointed, but another day was to come when our boys successfully attacked the Tans in Abbeyfeale, as planned.

Some time later, as we still remained billeted in the neigh-bourhood, we were very much disappointed to learn that a patrol arrived at Meenahela creamery, having travelled on bicycles from the town, a distance of approximately five miles. Our scouts routed us out of our beds to inform us of their presence so close at hand but we could do nothing to prevent their departure. Anyway we would not attack in the vicinity of the creamery because the building would surely have been burned out and the people living within a radius of three miles or more would be deprived of their source of income.

I can best remember the farmhouse I slept in belonging to a family called the Patsy Toms. There I had the most comfortable bed that ever came my way at that time. I slept with an old man, Tom, and actually revelled in the comfort the bed provided; a four poster timber one, made up of a grand feather mattress, real good blankets, a homemade quilt and no sheets. Staying on for my dinner of heavy fat bacon, potatoes and a plentiful supply of cabbage, it astonished the family that I could not eat it. Then I was asked to eat a couple of duck eggs, instead of the bacon which I had to refuse as my insides revolted at the fare so generously given. Fat bacon did not appeal to many of us at that time but exceptions were to be found. One of the boys, J. J., never refused to eat it and the fatter the better. The town boys would not touch it, and J. J. was subjected often to sly hints about his capacity to eat it with genuine relish. Jerry Moloney, a member of our column, was particular as to his diet and unless butchers' meat was provided he would not touch bacon under any circumstances. It can be understood that the countryman's diet consisted almost exclusively of bacon. On one occasion when the column was billeted near the Kerry–Cork border a farmer's wife invited all to partake of salted beef—a rarity, to be sure.

It happened that her husband was after slaughtering a cow which had fallen into a ditch and broken a couple of her legs. Whether it was properly cured or not, the eating of it caused many a sore stomach and painful diarrhoea. Jerry had a good laugh at the boys' expense as he himself never touched the meat. He dined on eggs, bread, butter and tea. He saw the spectacle of twenty men relieving themselves behind a fence simultaneously. I can tell you he enjoyed himself immensely.

During April and May significant reorganisation took place all over our area. It was then that Battalion Flying Columns were formed. Each company supplied the best of their men for this purpose. My Battalion Vice Commdt., Jimmy Collins, was appointed its Commander. The old column representing the brigade was disbanded. Into each of the new battalion Active Service Units (A.S.U.) were placed members of the old column so as to give the new battalion units confidence from those already having experience in various fights with the enemy. In West Limerick we had five columns, each column to carry on the war in its own area. This change did not mean that all enrolled in these units had to sleep away from home each night. The officers in charge being "on the run", could not do this and were engaged whole time in training the new force; they spent their time at each centre and moved from company to company. One of our main worries was shortage of rifles; on the formation of these battalion units their shortage was most apparent. Strengthened by about six rifles each column depended for the greater number on shotguns and a few bombs; in fact rifles were like gold to us right up to the end of the conflict.

Just as these columns were formed I found myself in the Mount Collins area. Dinny Lane, the company officer, and some others, myself included, were one day relaxing in Lane's farmhouse when we were rudely disturbed by a noise emanating from motor trucks and coming closer to us each minute. Seizing our guns, we ran out the back door into a field at the rear and there we took shelter. We saw the military trucks drive past Lane's, and on reaching a house about three hundred yards further on they slowed down and stopped. We saw an officer and some soldiers leave their trucks and enter the house. After a short time they came out, rejoining their companions, then seated themselves in their cars and drove off. If this had been a raid on Lane's farmhouse or the usual search we might not have escaped the notice of the military so easily. The sole purpose of their visit was to secure possession of a Lee-Enfield rifle held by a member of the household. The owner of the rifle was an ex-British officer who was married to a daughter of W. Cahill, whose house had just been visited. It appears that some member of Cahill's family had notified the military authorities at Newcastle West of their wish to hand over to them possession of this gun.

It was galling to Dinny Lane that a near neighbour could not see his way to give his rifle to the I.R.A. I am sure W. Cahill would have done so, reluctantly, if he knew what his action was going to cost him before many hours had passed. The aftermath was that I convened a military court of three officers, presided over by myself, which reached a decision unanimously, that this man be fined a sum of fifty pounds to be paid immediately to the I.R.A. funds. Dinny Lane and myself notified him of our verdict and to our amazement he handed us fifty pounds right away. This was a large sum at that time, or any other, to extract from any man. Collecting these fines was not always so easy to accomplish at that time. We, the I.R.A., quite independent of the Sinn Féin courts, held our own military courts on members, for various reasons from refusal to carry out orders, insubordination, fighting and breaches of discipline.

Dinny Lane, a Volunteer named Johnny, and myself, went one evening to a farmer's place to collect a fine imposed by Dinny on a young Volunteer who refused to obey orders. When we arrived to collect the fine (£5), we were attacked by the farmer and his son, who, armed with a pitchfork and spade handle, tried to do us bodily harm. Our Volunteer, Johnny, a powerful young man, in a fierce struggle and after receiving a few wounds, disarmed his opponent. Dinny and myself battled to bring peace between us and calm down the father and son. We did not succeed but Capt. Lane, seeing that no cash would be paid, seized on whatever goods he thought would be valued at £5 or thereabouts. We escaped out of the place, lucky to be sound in limb, but with a black eye and some skin peeled off in the encounter. Incidents such as I have related were of frequent occurrence and did not enhance the reputation of the I.R.A., but in a few short months would bear their own bitter fruit in the turmoil of the Civil War.

The I.R.A. men were often asked to do daft things by their civilian friends. Whilst in the Templeglantine area I was approached by a young attractive girl, accompanied by a friend, to do something that the priest of the parish himself would not dare to do. This was nothing short of a request that I compel a certain young farmer into a forceable marriage with her. She explained her reasons for this, stating that he fathered her still unborn babe and that she'd swear in any court of the land that she spoke the gospel truth regarding their courtship and the number of times spent at their lovemaking. Whilst feeling sorry at her unpleasant state I had to firmly inform her that the business was outside my jurisdiction.

Sinn Féin courts sometimes had to deal with broken promises and the unhappy consequences of passionate love affairs. Unhappy marriages were common in rural Ireland. Sometimes warring couples presented their viewpoints and aired their dirty linen before Sinn Féin courts. At these courts, some inveterate gossips attended to chew on the unsavoury titbits brought to light around their circle of cronies.

Once again I paid a flying visit to my wife's home on the Listowel–Ballybunion road. My visits were of short duration as it was a dangerous locality with constant enemy movement every day on this road. Sleeping there one night with Paddy Walsh as companion, we were startled next morning to see from our bedroom window a Crossley tender filled with Tans stop at the gate and from it jumped onto the road a few of them. They came along outside my room and walking quickly entered the kitchen. Everyone was frightened at seeing them so close at hand as the name they bore and their savagery were well known. This morning they behaved in an exemplary manner, requesting the use of a bucket to get some water from the pump nearby, and after a short time departed. I can tell you that I was in no bed of roses whilst they stayed around.

In North Kerry I met the column operating there under Commdt. Denis Quille. One morning after breakfast I sauntered out into a field beside the road where Paddy Walsh was busily ploughing. As I walked up and down the newly turned sods and watched the earth being exposed to the light and the sun, hundreds of gulls swooped down in a noisy screaming swarm to fill their gullets with the exposed worms, devouring them to satisfy an unsatiable appetite. This peaceful scene was violently disrupted by outbursts of gunfire and rifle fire from some place near at hand. Paddy and I stood there in a daze at such an unexpected occurrence. On his advice I set about getting away before any reprisal took place but before I could put into action my intention of leaving, what did we see but an armed party of North Kerry men retreating down the road towards us. They came to a halt on the road outside Walsh's farmhouse where I contacted them. From what I could gather they were just after ambushing a police patrol at Liselton Railway Station (on the old Lartigue line). It appeared as if it was an inconclusive fight, for both parties called off the engagement after a short time. When the police force was not wiped out by the first I.R.A. gunfire it gave the police a chance to seek shelter behind banks and hedges. A long drawn out fight would not have suited the column, as the fight was on the main road, only four miles from reinforcements; hence their withdrawal.

My next visit to Kerry was one I'll long remember. On 12 May three I.R.A. men belonging to No. 1 Kerry Brigade were captured and shot down in cold blood, at a place called Knockanure, well known in song and story for many a day. The young men captured and shot were returning to their district in North Kerry after attending a retreat at the parish church in Athea, some three miles inside the Limerick border. They were four in number, namely Con Dee, Paddy Dalton, Jerry Lyons and Paddy Walsh. As they sauntered along a sheltered byroad coming to a little bridge spanning a mountain stream at Gortaglanna they rested a while before continuing westwards.

This bridge at Gortaglanna was situated in a secluded hollow and one could see for a distance this glen opening to the south. As the bridge held a commanding position one could see down through scattered trees and tangled growth where the stream cascaded as it tumbled downwards to join the Feale river. Looking in any other direction one's view was restricted to about a couple of hundred yards as the ground rose rapidly towards the north, east and west. It happened that the four young men were roused to danger by the sudden appearance on the brow of the road leading to Listowel of a Crossley tender filled with Black and Tans. They got little time to effect their escape as the Tans encircled them almost at once. Marching their four prisoners before them up the Listowel road they arrived at a crossroad leading to Knockanure, up which their captors moved them. They halted, ordered their prisoners inside the roadside fence and placed them in a line, some few yards from the road but facing it. Leaning on the bank with their rifles pointed at the prisoners the Tans immediately shot them down in cold blood.

Miraculously, Con Dee escaped; on the order to fire he ran headlong towards the bank on which the Tans were taking aim. His unbelievable escape was the talk of North Kerry and West Limerick people for many a long day. Pursued by some of the Tans, Con was severely wounded by being shot through the thigh. After running a considerable distance he collapsed from loss of blood and fell into a boggy ditch in a desperately bad state. The Tans finally withdrew, taking the bodies of their victims with them to the police station in Tralee. The bodies received scant attention—thrown on the floor of the Crossley tender with their heads and legs hanging out at the back and blood stained features—in a heap together. It was a terrible sight to see. People living near Knockanure heard the shooting and wondered at it.

A farmer, Bill Sullivan, in whose land Con Dee was eventually discovered, brought him to a farmhouse in a townland called Larrha at O'Conners. There Julia, my wife, and myself visited him on the evening of that day—these murders brought sorrow to three families. Dr. Enright, from Listowel, was summoned to Con's bedside to examine and treat his wounds. Both Dr. Enright and my wife, a nurse, attended him regularly until he was out of danger. Con Dee gave me a firsthand account of Gortaglanna and its tragic ending for three young men at the hands of a murderous foe. It is true to relate that three of the boys were blood relations of my wife.

The brave Cumann na mBan from Listowel and nearby districts travelled to Tralee barracks to demand the remains. Under the eyes and hostile demeanour of the police and military, these girls carried out the funeral arrangements and brought back to Listowel Railway Station the mortal remains in three coffins covered with the flag of the Irish Republic. Those three died as martyred soldiers in the cause of freedom.

After parting from Con Dee and my wife at that farmhouse in Larrha, a few miles from the Shannon, I made my way home, calling at Con Brosnan's in Moyvane. Con Brosnan, an officer in his local company I.R.A., was in later years one of the foremost footballers on the Kerry All-Ireland team. From Con I secured a bicycle to take my feet off the road and on it I cycled to John Leahy's, Dromodda, a distance from Moyvane of about six miles. There I left the bicycle, to be returned to its owner as soon as convenient. At this time darkness was over the land and I still had to travel over ten miles of a mountain and cross some streams and rivers before reaching my destination. I was advised at Leahy's not to travel by road but to take to the fields, as patrols of the enemy were regularly seen on the roads at night as they silently marched along on the green margin by the roadside. After a hasty cup of tea I set out on my journey, crossing over a high hill called Knocknaboul and made my way as best I could in the semi-darkness of an early summer night.

I traversed through bogland, scarred by cuttings made to provide turf for winter use. I had some escapes from these as I was wary of falling into bog holes and the wetting I'd get as a result made me very cautious. It took me some time on this lonely mountain, alone as I was, before I crossed over its brow and descended its other side onto the road between Athea and Abbeyfeale. I crossed over this road conscious of the military patrols using it. Once over I made my way up a steep road near Cratloe creamery and never halted until reaching the home of Jimmy Leahy, an I.R.A. officer, living in a district called Ballaugh. There I rested for about two hours and after that made my way to a farmhouse owned by Michael Leahy in the townland of Ballycommane. During the night I had travelled about twenty miles or so to reach it. It was of utmost importance to me to be at Leahy's farm on that particular day. The reason being that the house was used as a rendezvous where Liam Lynch, Commdt. 1st Southern Division, and his

Adjutant, Commdt. Florrie O'Donoghue, were to meet me. Hence my trek over bog and mountain to attend there punctually. The meeting had been arranged some days previously— on instructions from our Brigade Commdt. Garrett McAuliffe I was to meet these officers and bring them to "Hayes", Glenagown, a sheltered farmhouse on the hillside looking down on Newcastle West.

A brigade council was summoned, comprising the battalions—five in number—at least two or more officers would attend representing their battalions. The brigade staff was also present and all were anxious to hear what Liam had to say. Only lately were the brigade areas in South Munster united under Liam Lynch and known as the 1st Southern Division I.R.A. The purpose of the commanding officer was to get acquainted with each brigade staff, listen to what they had to say, and try to coordinate activities into a uniform pattern all over the region. Later this was implemented in West Limerick but for various reasons could not be carried out simultaneously as planned.

I am afraid I am anticipating things, so will start on that meeting with Liam Lynch and Florrie O'Donoghue. On my arrival at Mick Leahy's introductions were made to vouch for our identities. After a quick repast we set out on our journey to Hayes's, approximately eight miles. We were each armed with a rifle and ammunition. Leaving Ballycommane townland behind us we tramped over some rough pastureland, crossed the local river at "Barber's Bridge", then had a stiff climb over land and hedges until reaching the summit of a range of high, heather-clad hills extending for miles to the east. These hills separated Templeglantine from Tournafulla and we had a pleasant surprise on reaching the top. From here could be seen the valley extending to the Shannon river on the western horizon and the scenic panorama which embraced the Galtees to the east over rolling hills on to the Kerry range from Mt. Brandon to the Gap of Dunloe. On our journey Liam Lynch expressed his pleasure as he viewed the scene of the rolling hills, the valleys, and streams to the west and the rich green land of the Limerick plain. It was a glimpse of scenic beauty in a time of war.

On our march we kept to the top of these hills until reaching Barna Gap then crossed the road beside the railway station. Liam Lynch was pleasantly surprised to meet an acquaintance coming off the afternoon train. We traversed the main road for about a mile keeping a sharp look out for the enemy, our view being restricted by high banks, trees and hedges. We got through successfully to our destination at Hayes's farmhouse.

On our arrival discussions began on the problems that affected us in West Limerick. Liam Lynch outlined for us a proposal he believed would cause concern to the enemy and puzzlement also. This was that a simultaneous attack on the enemy be carried out against them in the principal towns of West Limerick. This proposal was agreed on and the battalion commdts. said they would do everything possible to make it a reality. After the council had agreed to do the best they could they adjourned to meet again when necessary. I got a pony and trap ready for Liam Lynch and Florrie O'Donoghue to convey them to North Cork. Two Volunteers accompanied them, one being the driver of the vehicle. They conveyed them to Rockchapel on the Cork County border without incident of any sort.

During this month the Courthouse at Newcastle West was burned to the ground by a party of I.R.A. under the command of Garrett McAuliffe, Brigade O/C. This was a daring exercise as this building was situated quite close to the police barracks. Shortly after this event a surprise raid was carried out on the home of a suspected spy and collaborator living in Maiden Street. This street was in the heart of the town and great care was exercised in traversing the road leading to it. Arriving at their destination, around midnight, they knocked at the door which was opened within a few minutes. The inmates were frightened on seeing armed men invade their home and demand that the head of the house surrender to them. The suspected man jumped off his seat beside the fire, made a dash to the back door, opened it and as he was passing through was fired on by the I.R.A. He managed, though wounded, to stagger into the back garden and escaped over innumerable walls to safety.

Our boys dare not follow him into the maze of walls and wire fence enclosing the little patches of ground at the rear of Maiden Street. To follow this man would be suicidal as the police and military occupied buildings a few hundred yards away; if they heard any shots their source would lead to investigation. This surprise raid kept this man from having any further association with the Tans and soldiers stationed in Newcastle West. 'Spys Beware' was a warning that was heeded. Nothing would deter callous men from informing as the lure of large sums of money was a temptation they could not resist.

Shortly after this, information was brought to our brigade staff that a spy was at work in the 3rd Battalion area. Conclusive evidence was obtained to verify this news. Evidence was obtained in a letter addressed to the District Inspector of Police under a nom-de-plume, Mr. J. Ryan, c/o Post Office, where his letters were to be called for. It happened there was another J. Ryan who, on his visits to the Post Office on business, asked the postmistress if any letters had come for him. On this day he got some letters; amongst them was one that shook his composure. After reading its contents he closed it as well as he could and handed it back to the post office official, then quickly made his way to a prominent Sinn Féiner and disclosed to him the contents of the letter. This person came to our headquarters and told us the contents of the letter, which were of a very incriminating nature.

It was vital to secure this letter immediately so Lieutenant Paddy Aherne volunteered to cycle four miles into town where this Post Office was situated. Aherne arrived safely although the town was patrolled by Black and Tans. No notice was taken of him so by luck and courage he succeeded in his objective. At the Post Office he demanded this special letter from the postmistress. She refused to give it. As Paddy was not to be put off he pulled a revolver from his pocket and pointed it at her and threatened to shoot her if she did not comply with his request. Reluctantly the letter was handed over to him, then leaving the Post Office quite calmly he mounted his bicycle and his luck held—no policeman even looked at him as he passed by.

On Paddy's arrival at Brigade H.Q. the contents of the letter were revealed which said that the District Inspector of Police was ready to pay out a large sum of money for information leading to the capture or destruction of the North Cork Flying Column, billeted quite near the Cork–Limerick border. This letter revealed the name of the informer and the final acceptance of a large sum of money to be paid to him for this information. This spy was arrested, sentenced to death and executed.

Now that battalion columns were formed it was urgent that some action be taken against the Crown Forces in all areas. Our battalion council discussed the matter and decided, once again, to bring in help to aid us in attacks and ambushes. As a result of our meeting and to give effect to its decision, I, with their approval, travelled to Meelin, Co. Cork and contacted the North Cork men at Twomey's farmhouse. This farmhouse was a fine structure built with limestone, hewn by hand, and situated in pleasant surroundings. In the large dining-room were assembled a number of armed men relaxing for the time being.

I introduced myself to them and stated to Commdt. Michael O'Sullivan, one of their officers, what my errand was: namely an attack on the Tans at Abbeyfeale. They agreed that help would be given and a day named when they would meet me and others of our column at Barretts, Meenahela. Having outlined for them the daily habits of the Tans in and outside the town it looked possible that a position I had selected close to Abbeyfeale would suit the purpose. To vex and irritate the Tans we had posters printed and pasted to walls, telegram poles and other places. The printed matter was uncomplimentary and rude with strong language to infuriate them. Everywhere they saw these posters they tore them down; at night our Volunteers pasted them up again—they suffered the same fate.

On the arranged night about twenty men from North Cork under brigade officer Paddy O'Brien arrived at Barretts. I and about ten of our battalion active service men awaited their arrival. After eating at Barretts we all moved and marched to Abbeyfeale, about four miles. Moving silently on the grass margins we moved into four farmhouses beside the ambush position overlooking the town, a distance of about a half-mile. Resting uneasily until dawn and then in its obscure light we made our way into the positions chosen to await impatiently the arrival of the Tans. There we stayed until ten o'clock when we saw the police, about ten in number, leave their barracks and march along the Newcastle West road, pulling down our notices as they moved along. They continued on this road until well clear of the town, then returned to the town square, into the road leading to our positions on a steep hill. Everyone looked to his weapons to make certain that they were service-able. The Tans came to within 300 yards of us, stopped for a while and seemed uncertain what to do, then, to our terrible disappointment, turned about and marched back to their barracks. It was a grievous blow to us and to our comrades from County Cork considering their long tramp to Abbeyfeale and their tiresome march back to Rockchapel where they rested. Before leaving our positions another night had fallen to cover our retreat. Any movement in daylight stood a chance of being seen by the police from their barracks, as it stood at the foot of the hill we had occupied, and if field glasses were used by them they would surely expose us to their gaze.

We were in great danger, for if this police garrison contacted the military in Newcastle West or Tralee, we'd be in a dangerous situation of being surrounded and our retreat a hazardous undertaking. The North Cork men rested at Rockchapel for a week and ours at Mt. Collins to try to again attack the enemy if possible. Well, it was deemed not possible so the North Cork men moved into their own area, but did come to our aid early in July.

During this time the I.R.A. Column of the 3rd Battalion occupied houses in Dromcollogher and successfully ambushed the Tans. In charge were Con Foley, Batt. O/C., Ben Sullivan, Vice-O/C., and around twenty men. They occupied houses in the town and early one morning in May when the police were passing by they opened heavy fire on them with rifles and shotguns. In the exchange of fire one policeman was killed and several others seriously wounded as they retreated in haste back to their barracks. None of the attacking force was injured. On the withdrawal of the police our boys came onto the streets and carried away the weapons abandoned by the Tans in their flight back to the barracks.

Dromcollogher suffered severely the following night from reprisals carried out by drunken Tans and military who ran wildly through the streets, firing shots and throwing bombs indiscriminately. It was with great reluctance the I.R.A. men left the town as they felt it was their duty to protect the townspeople who invariably suffered from these reprisals. It would take great courage and planning, together with a strong armed force, to bring to a halt such reprisals. Ben Sullivan, who was born and reared there, felt it could be done. He knew every lane and alleyway and believed that if fire was opened on the rampaging mob of police and soldiers it would curb such brutalities and compel them to defend themselves instead of terrorising helpless people.

Following the foregoing events I decided, after consulting our battalion officers Jimmy Collins, P. J. O'Neill, Johnny Harnett and Jerry Moloney, that the only way to get at the Tans in Abbeyfeale was by occupying houses in the town. On the morning of 5 June, around 4 a.m., about twenty men arrived on the outskirts from Newcastle Road. Scouts met our party there and moving in front of the attacking party, all in bare feet, guided a selected party of eight men to the houses to be occupied. Shortly afterwards the rest of the column moved into Abbeyfeale, also in bare feet, to occupy houses converging on the square. During the night the offensive notices were again put up—ordering the Tans to leave the country and containing nice comments on the police force and on their ancestry. One notice was posted on the very door of the barracks that morning by Volunteers Thomas O'Connell and P. Collins, a really daring act.

Where the town square converged on two roads a large telegraph pole stood and on it were plastered several of these offensive notices. We believed the police would certainly stop at this pole and probably congregate there as they usually did and pull down these abusive posters. At about 6 a.m. the Tans discovered it on their own doorstep, then moved up the town in extended formation, about twelve men armed with rifles and revolvers. On coming to the notices stuck on the pole they halted and were about to tear them down when a whistle was blown, to be followed immediately by gunfire from our party. This was directed at the Tans from the houses on the square. Taken completely by surprise, the Tans paused for a moment, then dashed in headlong flight back to the shelter of their barracks, some firing their weapons aimlessly as they ran. Our party kept up their fire and one of the Tans was seen to fall mortally wounded and others were also injured. Constable Jolly fell in the first fusillade near the telegraph pole—the decoy used by our boys to lure them into the trap set for their destruction. After the flight of the Tans our boys came onto the streets and collected the abandoned weapons, then in orderly fashion retreated from the town under the command of Jimmy Collins, who earlier had led the advance party to occupy the houses. No casualties were incurred by our party in this engagement.

In a rapid march our boys placed several miles between them and Abbeyfeale and billeted in houses in a safe locality protected by guards and scouts. The Tans did not leave their barracks for a considerable time after our party had left. They then came on the streets and fired several volleys through every road in the town. Some policemen acted so violently that they had to be restrained by their officers and companions. They raided every house whose occupants were known to have sympathy with the I.R.A. and those houses where some of the members were in the Republican Army. It was a frightening day for the townspeople as they listened to the uproar made by the rampaging Tans and military reinforcements that had arrived to terrorise them.

Jamsie D. Harnett, a newspaper reporter for *The Kerryman* at that period, wrote the following of this event:

Early in the morning of the fifth of June, 1921, a second ambush took place in Abbeyfeale, and a Black and Tan named Jolly was killed and several others wounded. When the I.R.A. withdrew from the town many of the inhabitants had narrow escapes from being shot. Head Constable Casey saved the writer from a Black and Tan named Nolan, who, seemingly insane, discharged his rifle repeatedly into the wall of Jimmy Joy's house before being disarmed by his comrades. He was carried away, still shouting in frenzy that he would have revenge for his chum Jolly.

From time to time I visited my parents' home to get clean underwear and for a chat, usually ending with advice to keep out of danger and an expression of their belief that it was all madness, this idea of winning a fight against the might of England. I also paid visits to my Aunt Mary and old Jack Wrenn, the workman in Killaculleen. Nearby was Mrs. Kelly's farmhouse where I and some of the boys often stayed. Sleeping there one night on makeshift beds in the parlour was John Joe Leahy, J. Collins and myself. During the night I smelt smoke and rousing the others we investigated and discovered the smoke was coming from a room occupied by the servant girl. Opening the door we saw the bedclothes smouldering around the occupant; it was caused by an overturned lighted candle beside the bed. Only for our quick intervention the poor girl would have been burned to death and the whole thatched farmhouse as well.

A short time after this J. Joe Leahy and myself were again at Mrs. Kelly's; this time I myself was seriously ill, suffering from rheumatic fever. Mrs. Kelly's son, a young doctor, Denis Kelly, treated me and I remember well the large glass of rum I drank, the first in my life, to induce a semi-intoxicated sleep that eased my pains somewhat. Unfortunately I could not stay at Kelly's because of enemy searches; though very ill I was removed to another farmhouse about a mile away. In this house I was placed in a room with an earthen floor, in a large timber bed occupying one corner of the room. In the other corner there was a large heap of potatoes giving out a penetrating obnoxious odour from the fungus-like growth of the spuds, completely preventing me from getting either rest or sleep. The heat of summer and the damp earthen floor combined to induce a revulsion in me against such an environment. Praying for the morning light to give me an excuse to leave, I bade the family farewell and got a welcome in another farmhouse in the same townland. There I spent a few weeks during very warm weather, gradually recovering from rheumatic fever until I was well again.

After recovering from my illness, plans were made to ambush British military and police regularly using the road between Newcastle West and Abbeyfeale. Their numbers were usually around sixty men travelling in Crossley tenders preceded by a private car containing their officers. They usually drove in extended order with a good distance between each vehicle for safety reasons.

Once again I paid a visit to North Cork where I met the officers and men of the flying column at Rockchapel, near the Limerick border. Commdts. P. O'Brien and Mick Sullivan and some others agreed to come to our area and study and examine suitable positions with me. A good deal of this month of June was given over to this planning and examination of suitable ambush positions. Commdt. Mick Sullivan, known as "red haired Mike", spent a few weeks in West Limerick with me surveying the country around Templeglantine. Mike Sullivan was a fine handsome man, cool and calm, very studious and never without a good book to read in times of relaxation.

One day Mike and myself had come over the hills from Tournafulla and were coming down to the main road near Templeglantine Church conversing together and not very watchful of where we were heading. On going through the yard of a farmhouse owned by a family named Sexton our progress was interrupted by one of the Sexton girls, who pointed down towards the road beneath us, about three hundred yards away, and said: "don't ye see the soldiers? Ye'll be killed if ye cross the fields as the soldiers will see ye armed with rifles as ye are." You may be sure we paused and looking over the yard fence perceived a large number of military in extended formation traversing the roads and fields in the valley beneath us. There seemed to be hundreds of them searching houses and fences over a large area of Templeglantine district and also interrogating everyone they met. It looked like an encircling movement from which we so narrowly escaped. Turning around we retraced our steps, taking off our jackets as we did so. Placing them on the butts of our rifles, we put the guns on our shoulders with the jackets hanging off them to give the appearance of hayforks on our shoulders as if going hay-making. As we retraced our steps back up the hillside our composure was somewhat shaken when an aeroplane swooped down low as it flew over us; it repeated this exercise a couple of times. We were glad when we crossed the crest of the hill and were out of sight of soldiers and aeroplane.

After passing over the brow of this hill we had to traverse a very bare black stretch of mountain bogland with no cover of any kind for about a mile. At the foot of this hill was a road without a hedge of any kind for a couple of miles affording us no cover as we walked along until reaching a little cabin owned by Batt Wrenn, an old bachelor living alone. He made us a cup of tea as we rested for a little while before we continued on to Mrs. Kelly's—some distance in from the road. There the Kelly girls made us welcome and we stayed the night. Next day we again went down to Templeglantine and examined likely ambush positions from Barna to Devon Road with the possibility of a train attack in the same district. Here the railway line ran between Limerick and Tralee; it was used at that time by parties of military travelling between both garrison towns. We had to abandon the idea of an attack on military travelling by train as they were intermixed with civilians and never used this means of transport as a troop train. This left us with the road, as here they travelled regularly in convoys of Crossley tenders and these usually carried approximately fifty men or more.

We spent all the end of June in gathering information about the enemy and their use of the road, assessing the pros and cons of various ambush sites, the signalling, scouting, and outposts necessary to provide the maximum protection against surprise or against reinforcements. Commdt. Paddy O'Brien, Mike Sullivan and other I.R.A. officers finally agreed on what seemed the best ambush position near Templeglantine Church.

During the summer of 1921, before the Truce, some of our column arrested a suspicious looking young man near the Kerry–Limerick border. After searching him and on discovering some incriminating correspondence on his person, they brought him to me for interrogation. The letters revealed that he was lately demobbed from the British Army and also that he was a native of the Tralee district. He had on him evidence that he was collaborating with the police force in Tralee and that he had already given evidence in court there, behind a wire netting to conceal him from the prisoners against whom he was giving evidence, to help convict them to long prison sentences or worse. I secured a photo of him in military uniform, a private in the Munsters. Contacting the Tralee I.R.A., I duly handed over our prisoner to them.

On a similar occasion, some of our boys of the flying column were staying in houses not far from Abbeyfeale in the Dromtrasna district. They captured a Black and Tan who had left his barracks in Abbeydorney, North Kerry, some days previously. Humphrey Murphy, Commdt. East Kerry Brigade I.R.A., alerted us about him. I received a dispatch from this officer about his absence from his barracks, giving a description of this Tan, and emphasizing that he had a great thirst. Our boys disarmed him and placed him under an armed guard at the farmhouse of Dinny McEnery. His name was Crosseley and I remember him as being tall, of strong build, dark complexion with a pimply, ruddy face. We discovered he was a native of Dungannon, a Protestant of indifferent piety; religion was not a burning question with him. His thirst was an overpowering urge, to be satisfied at all costs. The officer in Kerry who sent me the dispatch remarked indifferently in his letter, "you can do what you like with him". This meant literally—shoot him if you think fit—but I was not quite prepared to carry out this drastic proposal. Before our battalion staff could decide his fate or meet to discuss the problem he created, he made a dash for freedom when out in the field for exercise, near where he was incarcerated with two armed guards in attendance. Called on to halt by his guards he ignored their warning. It was only after a chase and the firing of a couple of shots at him that he halted with hands uplifted to denote surrender.

After this incident it was decided that an armed guard and myself convey him by car to the H.Q. of the First Southern Division at Lombardstown in Co. Cork. We agreed to leave his fate in their hands. On arrival there I met Brigadier Tom Barry and Tom Daly, Adjutant of the Division and told them my problem. They accepted responsibility for the future of my prisoner but Tom Barry remarked "Why did you not drop him into a bog hole on your way here?"

One Sunday afternoon I visited Volunteer J. Leahy at his home at the western end of our parish. Sitting out beside a sheltered bank, on its sunny side, we were chatting about events and the effects the summer weather was having on our campaign. Some columns at that time were sleeping out under hedgerows in beds of hay and felt safer there than in houses. Dugouts were still unheard of in the South and only came into use as a dire necessity during the Civil War.

Lying there at our ease we were suddenly startled by the sound of gunfire towards the east. This continued for a time and ceased as suddenly as it started. We moved instinctively towards the sound of the gunfire, and traversed across the fields, keeping in the shelter of the hedges and furze growing on the high banks. We came to Knocknadiha hill looking down on the road near Sullivan's cottage and the nearby schoolhouse. Seeing nothing of a suspicious nature on the road below us, we enquired of a neighbour living nearby what was the cause of the shooting. He informed us that earlier on a couple of tenders filled with military passed along the road and drove blindly into trenches cut in the road near Sullivan's cottage. These trenches were cut in a dip on the road and could not be seen from a fast moving vehicle. At that time some of the boys of the column were at the cottage getting their boots repaired. They were Martin Ward, Captain Jackie Sullivan, and Aeneas Sheehan, Adjt. 2nd Battalion.

On hearing the crash made by the lorry as it struck the trench they ran out of the cottage and up a high boreen to a high bare hill leading upwards. As they ran they were observed by the soldiers who opened fire and pursued them for a good distance, firing all the time. Aeneas Sheahan broke away from them and ran at right angles inside a hedge and escaped though bullets cut the ground beside him. Up straight, the high hill before them, ran Martin Ward and Jackie Sullivan with soldiers close behind them. Coming to a sod fence they both crossed it like hounds and found themselves in a field filled with tall rushes. Martin threw himself on the ground and wriggled his way into a dense growth of rushes, without being seen. Jackie was not so lucky. As he had just started to imitate Martin, a soldier with his rifle pointed at him called on him to surrender as he stood on the fence looking down at him. So started for him a long period of trial and hardship. He was taken to Newcastle West with Mick Sullivan, one of the Sullivan family. On their journey they were subjected to cruelties and abuse and in the castle yard that night their lives were threatened. Jackie Sullivan was caught with arms and on a Sam Brown belt he wore was printed his name and rank of Captain I.R.A. Mick Sullivan was released but Jackie had to stand trial for his life and was defended by O'Brien Moran, Solicitor, Limerick. He was lucky that the truce of 11 July put a stop to his possible execution.

Towards the end of June, some members of the Templeglantine Coy. I.R.A. felled some trees across the main road beside the Catholic church, completely blocking it to traffic. The following Sunday at Mass in the local church, the

Catholic curate made a scathing attack on the I.R.A. for obstructing the road so near to the church and endangering it thereby from reprisals by the Tans, and abuse of the authority the I.R.A. held. He likened our activity to that of the Cromwellian hordes of former times and that we must be inspired by Viviani, an unscrupulous member of the French Cabinet at that time. "I am sure", said he, "the next thing to happen will be that the I.R.A. will knock down the church and place it across the road!"

This tirade was reported to me by the local Coy. Captain Tom Sexton, demanding an apology and retraction of the curate's uncalled for statement at once. So, myself and three others (North Cork Volunteers) called at the Parochial House, knocked loudly at the door and demanded admittance in the name of the I.R.A. The curate answered our loud demand in person, heard our demand for retraction of the statements he made about us from the altar of God and that the privilege it afforded him was abused by him. I cannot now recall if we got our request granted. Our forces may have been wrong in felling trees in proximity to the church, but our action did not call for such an attack on us. Authority, lay or clerical, is always very touchy when anybody clashes with it.

We finally selected a position at Templeglantine, on the road to the east of the church, the Post Office and shop; about half a mile away from them. In preparation for this ambush we sent earlier in June two of our officers to the Forge in King Williams Town, Co. Cork to prepare mines which were to be used in the attack. There went Denis Collins and Larry E. Harnett and they spent a few weeks in that place being instructed in the making of explosives. The method to be used in filling iron pipes about two feet or so in height and a foot or more in diameter. They were trained in the placing of plates on top and bottom secured by strong bolts. They were also trained in the placing of detonators and they returned as qualified to do this work. A white powder, like flour, was used as the explosive substance; it was known as war flour.

The ambush position was a furze-covered fence running parallel to the road for over a half a mile or maybe more. It was distant from the road by about one hundred yards. At its eastern end where the road swung at a right angle the fence conveniently did so too thereby following the straight stretch of road to be engulfed by rifle and machine gun fire. This furze clad fence was well above the level of the road and except for a few short stretches one had a commanding view of the road. At the western end nearer to Abbeyfeale was a crossroads, and in between the main road and a byroad leading to the rear of the ambush position were a farmhouse, haybarn, cow byres and the usual farmyard buildings. Just across from these farm buildings was another byroad leading downwards to a small river and beside it some small houses and labourers' buildings. This farmhouse at the crossroads was protected by a strong whitethorn hedge, some trees and stone walls. It was proposed to place eight mines on the road at intervals along the ambush position, with wires attached to the detonators and controlled by a battery for each mine from inside the ambush position. Markers were placed on the roadside fence to indicate to the man operating the battery when the enemy vehicle was passing over the mine.

A good deal of organisation went into this work. It took time to get assembled around one hundred and twenty men from North Cork and West Limerick. In fact I think, now looking back, that we took so many elaborate pains to make our own plans foolproof that we defeated our purpose. We thought nothing was left to chance but luck was a fickle jade and did us a dirty turn. Our Cork I.R.A. column marched down to our headquarters at Mrs. Kelly's, Killaculleen, accompanied by signallers, scouts, engineers and first aid units. The mines were transported in a horse drawn cart and this column included a few horses for scouting and also some cyclists as dispatch riders. Halting at our village on their march on the evening of 8 July 1921, they got refreshments at the public houses there and never before or since was seen in Tournafulla such an armed party of Republican soldiers as thronged the place on that evening. Here was assembled upwards of sixty boys and men of that famous column who had fought so hard and won so many victories over our enemies during the two preceding years but not without losing some splendid young men killed in battle, executed or murdered by the savage Black and Tans.

It was a problem to billet all these men as a number of houses had to be requisitioned to accommodate such a large force. At headquarters the officers and engineers stayed with Mrs. Johanna Kelly before moving into the selected position. The rest of the column were accommodated in the neighbourhood touching on Templeglantine district. In Templeglantine the West Limerick column was billeted in houses extending westwards and north for a couple of square miles. At Mrs. Kelly's the boys enjoyed the company of four nice young girls who looked after their welfare and made it an occasion for jollification and fun always to be found amongst youngsters no matter how near danger lurked. The time of the Anglo-Irish War was no exception, so dancing, singing and a little courtship wherever the occasion offered was indulged in to the full. In retrospect:

> We remember the girls we kissed long ago.
> Where the Feale, the Shannon and Deel waters flow.

I must mention briefly my part in all the preparations made for the welfare and billeting of these I.R.A. men. It seems pointless to relate an undertaking which was a failure, but whether it was or not the utmost effort and energy had to be put into it, without making any reservations whatsoever about its ultimate end. In war all possible care should be made to see that success crowns the efforts of those engaged in attacks and surprise raids to gain them the maximum chance of achieving their objective. Despite every conceivable effort to leave nothing to chance it happens sometimes that some link in the chain breaks when never expected.

Our efforts at that time, coming so close to the Truce of 11 July 1921, were delayed longer than we expected. It was believed by all concerned, that is, our I.R.A. allies from North Cork and our own brigade staff that everything would be ready by 1 July at least. Well it did not work out that way and not until the 8th of the month was everything ready. It seemed pointless, coming so close to a Truce with the British, that lives might be lost as a result without any ensuing benefit. The deciding factor was that the achievement of a rather big victory, which we confidently expected, would win for us an honoured place in the I.R.A.

Well at last the morning dawned to give us light on our work as we marched that morning, 8 July. As we left our billets at around 4 a.m., it was one of the finest summer days I ever remember. We were in light-hearted humour as we moved along the road. We passed the old graveyard at 'Glantine, where we buried poor Liam Scully the year before. Coming along the road we contacted the Cork men moving out from Kelly's with their engineer section conveying mines on a cart. Now only the engineers, scouts, the vanguard of the column, about thirty to forty men, turned up a mountain road leading to Templeglantine and passing over the crest of this we could see all the big valley beneath us, with its main and by-pass roads and railway line. When our advance party tramped down this high road known as "The Lots Road" leading to a junction and the major road, we quickly moved along and at selected places started to dig holes for our eight mines. We had plenty of men to assist us at this mine laying; they covered the disturbed soil so that it seemed never to have been dis-turbed. The roads were not tarred at that time so we had plenty of whitish dust to camouflage our displaced road material. The wiring to the batteries was done efficiently and quickly. As we worked we heard in the distance the train approaching on its morning run from Tralee to Limerick. I can tell you we were not long in taking cover by the roadside fence until it had passed. Anybody travelling on the train had a good view of the road we were working on, as it was built on elevated ground and about three hundred yards away from us and was parallel to the road. Quickly our advance party made their way right up to our ambush position. Those with the Lewis gun made for the right angle bend to enfilade the road from there. Some Volunteers under the command of Michael Colbert were sent to occupy the houses near the little river about one hundred yards away from the road, to attack the enemy and prevent them from getting cover beside or inside the road fence visible to them.

The main command post at the right angle bend was occupied by Commandant Paddy O'Brien, Jim Brislane, Bill Moylan, Mike Sullivan and other officers. These men were in charge at selected posts over sections of rifle and shotgun men. Engineers were sent nearer to Newcastle West where they tapped the telegraph wires and set up a post connected to the command post where a listening device was set up to receive messages from them regarding the strength of the enemy travelling towards our ambush point, and also to send warning of reinforcements. By morning around 7 a.m. the greater number of our troops were just settling down in their positions and others were approaching down the hill at our back and still a good distance to our rear. But before final instructions could be given we heard in the distance the sound of motor vehicles approaching from the Newcastle West direction. Before we realised what was happening, on they came with a private car in the front followed by four transport Crossleys filled with troops and they drove quickly over our mined road and disappeared in the direction of Abbeyfeale.

Then the remainder of our men came and occupied the posts to carry out the duties assigned to them. That crossroads with the farmhouse in the angle between the main and byroad was an important defence and attack fortress and there some of our best West Limerick men were posted. If at this point the enemy should penetrate up the byroad it would leave our rear exposed and retreat route also. From this junction the West Limerick column line extended for a considerable distance to link up with the Cork column. Altogether about one hundred and twenty men with rifle and shotguns including engineers, scouts and signallers were assembled there and ready to carry out the commands of their officers.

There is one thing I think which militated against us and it is that our officers were really concerned about the strength of the military. They wanted visual evidence of their strength and so they were not exactly concerned on that first morning at seeing the enemy escape before our eyes. But I think once they knew the strength of the enemy they would feel more confident in attack as it was firmly believed by all of us that they would return by the usual route to Newcastle West. Well it did not happen and we spent three roasting days waiting for them from dawn through the night. The people living nearby fed us and each day brought us buckets of tea and bread and butter, which we consumed beside our positions. Each night we billeted in makeshift beds all round the district. At Kelly's house, Dan Vaughan, Bill Moylan and others from North Cork spent some lively nights. The early morning of 11 July came and we awaited news from Jerry Moloney and about a half-dozen men who entered Abbeyfeale during the night to attack any Tans who might appear on the streets, but none came out of their barracks. So our weary men returned to us at 'Glantine where we still stuck to our guns until about 12 noon, when the Truce with the British was to commence. All our boys were called together. We assembled on a gentle hillside overlooking our little river down below us in the valley. It was a truly lovely day of warm sunshine and it was a grand sight to see all the I.R.A. drawn up in two lines of armed men, some veterans of many a fight, others who were expecting their baptism of fire on the hills of West Limerick. Now all were somewhat disappointed at our recent failure to contact the enemy and felt deprived of the glory that an engagement would have shed on them. Anyway it would not have contributed any material advantage to the ultimate outcome, still mercifully hidden in the tragic future.

11 July 1921 was a fateful day in the history of Ireland and at 12 o'clock noon on that day was an event as significant as was the signing of the Treaty of Limerick two hundred and thirty years before. Both events recognised the existence of two armies, denied until now since that distant event of 1691.

One was the Army of Imperial England and ours was the legitimate Army of the Irish Republic. Remember too, this Truce was between two nations and not a portion of a dismembered country. But duplicity even in 1921 was the game, legitimate of course, as practised by our old foe. Hoodwink us! Of course they did. They established two states, one an accomplished fact even as they put out feelers to our government for the opening of negotiations between Ireland and England. Sad was the day for our people that we lost the war at the conference table. As the late Sean Moylan said, "We started this conflict with hurleys and finished it with fountain pens." Alas the pen was mightier than the sword. Many a fine Irishman has lost his life since that document was signed at the behest of David Lloyd George. Not by bullets fired by the British forces but by brother Irishmen. Never will we have peace whilst our ancient foe across the Irish Sea holds any portion of our land in bondage.

As our Republican troops stood arrayed that July day on an Irish hillside, it was really stirring to see them standing at attention with an assortment of guns and equipment, most of which had been captured from the Crown Forces. Beside them stood their own elected officers, their comrades all through the troubles. Addressing them in a farewell speech to mark the end of the phase of conflict was Brigade Commandant Paddy O'Brien, from Liscarroll, who had but lately stood in the place vacated by Sean Moylan (then a prisoner in the hands of the British). He reviewed all the important events of the past couple of years and the vital part of the Republican Army in it. He forecast that their services might once more be called upon to defend the rights of the Republic. Asking them to observe the Truce in a soldierly manner and that they be a credit to the country that bore them. So was dismissed one of the finest bodies of men ever before or since seen assembled on a green hillside or valley in Munster or in Erin.

After being dismissed the engineers had once again to disconnect their wired mines and dig up the road to unearth these engines of destruction. It is ironical to relate that whilst engaged at this work who should drive into our midst but a convoy of military from Newcastle West. These started to disarm the section who had remained to dismantle the mines. Despite protests the soldiers took their weapons to the barracks and some I.R.A. officers prevailed on the military to let them travel with them to Newcastle West where they retrieved their weapons from the superior officer there. So that evening began a trek in all directions by the I.R.A. to reach their homes and relatives. It was a long march for some to distant Charleville, Mallow, Ballydesmond, Newmarket, Lombardstown, Millstreet and Liscarroll in North Cork; Dromcollogher, Rathkeale, Pallaskenry, Glin, Ballyhahill, Newcastle West, Abbeyfeale and to every parish in West Limerick. It looked strange to Martin Ward and myself as we tramped back to our homes to see all round us farmers and their helpers being busily engaged in haymaking, as if nothing else mattered. From their peaceful occupation to our violent one a bond existed and without it we could not succeed. So this evening ended for us a phase in history which was unique and far reaching in its consequences.

On my arrival at my aunt's in Killaculleen on this July evening with Martin Ward we truly relaxed for the first time in many months. I put my weapons in a secure place: one a valuable weapon, a "Peter the Painter" automatic pistol; the other a Lee-Enfield .303 rifle. After we had had a cup of tea and a chat we crossed over the fields and river to the meadow where my father and his workmen were busy making whynds of hay. He did not greet us with any enthusiasm as he usually derided our efforts to free the country while he compared our equipment and organisation unfavourably versus that of the Empire. I am sure though that he must have felt that now probably it was all over, but not being given to any outward display of emotion or otherwise his cool reception of us, now at last free from looking over our shoulders, hid his relief that such was the case.

I parted from young Martin, then about seventeen years of age and recently promoted to be Adjutant of the 2nd

Battalion. He usually, owing to this post, was a close constant companion of mine. He established a headquarters wherever I was, and shortly after this time acquired a valuable typewriter and duplicating machine to help with documents sent out to Brigade H.Q. and coy. captains in our area. Leaving Martin to travel homewards, I called into my old home in Knocknadiha to see my mother and sister Mary. My two step-sisters, Bridie and Julia, were by this time married for some years. Bridie was married to a civil servant in Dublin named Pat Ingoldsby, who was at that time a friend of Arthur Griffith, President of Sinn Féin. Julia, a lovely, rather frail girl, was married to Michael Doyle, a Sergeant in the R.I.C. stationed at that time in Enniscorthy and later promoted to Head Constable in Ballyshannon.

I stayed that night and I can tell you I enjoyed a real relaxed sleep. Next day I cycled to Ballydonohue, near Ballybunion, to see my wife Julia and her relatives. Returning home I had to organise a battalion training camp in August at an empty mansion belonging to the late Miss Oliver, at Knocknabrack, a mile from Abbeyfeale. This was a spacious house in poor repair but it suited our needs. We had to get mattresses and bedding from our friends in town and country. We also had to provide rations each day for a large number of men. Fuel had to be provided. Volunteers did the cooking and all the utensils necessary had to be provided voluntarily.

Our training camp was run on real military lines. Regular hours, duly enforced, drill, gun practice and field manoeuvres and tactics. There were sentries posted day and night with passwords enforced and all out-of-bounds enforced rigidly. On our last day in the camp we had field exercises carried out on a large scale as we called in all the Volunteers in the Abbeyfeale Coy. I.R.A. to cooperate with us. John O', the caretaker at Miss Olivers, had a marvellous time during our stay there, as he was fed on food that in his wildest expectations he never dreamed he'd eat. He frequently came to thank me for our generosity to him; not that it cost us anything. One thing is certain, we had plenty of lice, and their kinfolk the flea took a hand during this warm August weather to remind us that they did not neglect their torment of us. At that time too the Republican itch was an additional torment and some boys suffered a good deal from its ravages as well as passing it on from every bed they slept in.

After this battalion training, undergone by the active service unit, we also had specialist training for our different services. These comprised of engineers, scouts, signallers, first aid, training of section leaders in their duties and detailing guards. A house in each coy. was selected for this training and there each morning assembled for instruction were the men selected. My home in Killaculleen was one of these houses and once again my aunt was kept busy for a fortnight looking after the needs of some dozen men. Our old workman Jack Wrenn, when not busy looking after the cattle, sat beside the fire and dozed off on a sugan chair with his faithful companion Charlie, a large collie dog, in his lap. He found amusement in the experiments of the boys although he was sceptical that their efforts would be successful. Captain Bill Horgan, a fine cool rugged young man, took calmly all things in his stride as he supervised the training.

The Truce between the British Government and Dáil Éireann brought its problems to both Sinn Féin and the I.R.A., both semi-independent of one another and who at this period were engaged in different work but for the same purpose, namely a free country. The flying columns, being as they were always on the move and on military duty, could not devote much time to the work Sinn Féin was engaged in. The I.R.A. believed that it was the tactics they carried out that put a halt to British rule in Ireland. It made them afterwards so reliant on force and on themselves as arbiters in our country's destiny. This is past history now and I will not resurrect its controversial consequences. During the period up to the Truce in 1921 hostility to the Republicans was kept below the surface owing to fear of the Volunteers—later the I.R.A. After the Truce things were never the same again, either for the ordinary person or for the I.R.A., but the uneasy peace was welcomed by all, and especially the people who had stood so nobly and unselfishly in giving unstinted help for the nation in dangerous times against brutal aggression.

The members of the flying columns, who had up to the Truce been mostly unknown to the British police, now felt free to appear openly, enter towns and mix with the public. By so doing they could no longer be anonymous citizens, so that the enemy had an advantage it never previously had. The I.R.A. were accorded first-class treatment in the towns and our town of Abbeyfeale was no exception. Some business people with munificent generosity kept them in their homes and feted them often at expense that some could ill afford. This was improving the morale of the "boys", who for so long endured the hard times of constant movement and danger so lately left behind them. After a month or so of this ideal relaxation, they were recalled to their various duties in their battalions, where training camps were established for intensive training, necessary if ever fighting broke out again.

In our area in West Limerick, the truce between the I.R.A. and the British forces was sometimes very hard to maintain. In the area of the Second Battalion, which included the town of Abbeyfeale, the Black and Tans were inclined to be very aggressive. In their patrols through the town they made it their business to push known sympathisers of ours off the pavements, abusing them as they did so. Things were getting so dangerous that there was a grave danger that armed attacks would be made on Tans because of their truculence. Something had to be done about it.

It was agreed by the battalion staff that Jimmy Collins, Vice Commdt., and myself should approach one of the Tan patrols on one of their periodic rounds. One evening, in fear and trepidation, we approached a patrol of Tans and R.I.C.— about eight in number—as they moved down the main street. We carried small arms hidden under our coats, and were covered by a party of our men who strolled down the opposite side of the street, well scattered so as not to attract attention. There was no public lighting then in Abbeyfeale, the only light being the light of paraffin lamps glowing weakly through shop windows.

As I accosted the officer of the patrol, an R.I.C. sergeant, they stopped in a somewhat irresolute manner, crowding around their officer as they listened to our conversation. I stated what our business was, and didn't mince my words about the conduct of their patrols on the street, saying that if they persisted in their behaviour some of his men would probably be shot. He listened to what I had to say, as he looked around apprehensively at his bunch of dangerous men. He was not too sure of their reaction to my accusations as they shuffled around uneasily with their weapons.

Giving an assurance that my complaints would be considered by his superior officer, the sergeant and his men moved off in the direction of their barracks. At their departure Jimmy Collins and myself breathed more freely; all the time we had realised the danger inherent in our abrupt confrontation with the patrol. After that things got quieter in Abbeyfeale, and an uneasy peace was maintained until the Treaty was signed.

The following is a copy of a dispatch I received in September at battalion headquarters. It was dated 24 September 1921 and shows the nervous tension in the Republican Army during the Anglo-Irish Truce, the period prior to the signing of the Treaty later that year:

(1) I have received instructions from the Liaison Officer that G.H.Q. are of the opinion that the "truce" is definitely drawing to an end.

(2) You will have all stuff dumped <u>at once</u> and have all men in your command in close touch with you.

(3) Starting on Monday you will send a dispatch rider from your Battalion G.H.Q. to Brigade H.Q. (T. Flynn's, Garrickerry) every day to arrive between the hours of 3 and 6 p.m.

(4) Keep this secret from the general public.

Signed O/C BGE.

Prior to receiving this order, members of the West Limerick Brigade column were enjoying a needed holiday in Ballybunion.

A very kind friend helped, by placing a large house at our disposal for the accommodation of around twenty men, together with cooking utensils, food and beds. The "boys" were assisted in the cooking by their girlfriends, and altogether we had a great time, swimming, dancing and with entertainment of various kinds. The nuns in the convent nearby gave a party in our honour and together, all of us, our girlfriends and some young priests we knew had a most enjoyable evening's entertainment there. Looking back now, I realise how wonderful was all the co-operation and kindness shown to us, really, because we did some bit for our country. We had this holiday after some weeks of strenuous training, spent in camps in different areas, and it was most welcome. It was, whilst in Ballybunion, that the dispatch came, notifying us of the possible ending of the Truce, and that hostilities could start at any time. The "boys", on learning of the urgency of the message, and a much regretted ending to our days of peace and joy in Ballybunion, manfully accepted the direful news, though saddened by the lamentations of their girl friends and wives. As many uncertainties always beset a soldier's life, it was doubly so, in the life of a guerrilla.

The Treaty, when signed in December, put "finis" for a time to further warfare, and then alas it was between ourselves, when the guns again spoke in anger. I remember well, prior to the departure of the Irish Delegates to the conference with the British Ministers, being at that time on a visit with Jimmy Collins to Dublin. Whilst there we called to see Batt O'Connor, who was a close friend of Michael Collins, and was of invaluable assistance to him. He had constructed a secret hiding place to keep twenty thousand sovereigns for Michael Collins as part of a fund to be used for the purpose of waging war on the British. It happened that on the evening we called to see Batt O'Connor, Michael Collins was also there and we all had tea together. During the evening various things were discussed and the occasion for Michael Collins was one of a farewell visit to his friend, as on the next day he was off to London to attend negotiations. I suppose he hoped for good wishes and encouragement from Batt, his intimate friend. Jimmy Collins, during our conversation with Michael Collins, asked him for his opinion on the negotiations about to take place. He was emphatic in his answer: "Nothing except a Republic will satisfy me!" It satisfied us too.

CHAPTER VI.

GREEN AGAINST GREEN, 1922.

After the Treaty was signed we all saw with joy and satisfaction the disbandment of the Black and Tans and Auxiliaries and their exodus from our land. During this period Michael Colbert, George Wallace and myself were returning to Limerick by train from Fermoy where we were at an officers training camp at Moorepark, just handed over by the military. We arrived at Limerick Railway Station carrying rifles and equipment and we were standing there awaiting the train to Tralee, when out of the blue and to our discomfiture and dismay about one hundred or so Black and Tans ran all over the place, jumping gates, shouting, whistling and acting like a mob bent on destruction.

When they saw us they gathered around us—some shouted "Here are the bloody Shinners!" "Here are some of the invisible army!" This was the first time we had met any of our opponents; before this we could never see them. Some shook us by the hand and said that at least they had met some I.R.A. men and could tell their friends about it. Some said they only wanted pay given them and that only necessity forced them to be in Ireland. Some were from as far away as Canada. They looked unkempt, unshaven, some under the influence of drink and all acted in the most unruly manner. The station master was distracted by their behaviour and was frantic with fear. In his distress he appealed to us for help, but it was like asking the blind to help the blind, as we were worried ourselves. The arrival of a large party of the old R.I.C. police force soon calmed the atmosphere and all was well again to our relief.

On the evacuation of the police barracks in Abbeyfeale and the military barracks in the Ellis mansion after the Anglo-Irish Treaty was signed and rather reluctantly ratified, our forces moved into these now vacant fortresses. In January 1922 I received an order from Commandant Garrett McAuliffe to occupy Abbeyfeale police barracks and place a maintenance party in it. I inspected the place and found that it was a very bare cold looking structure with the kitchen, dayroom, bedrooms and prison cells painted with the one colour, white limewash and limewashed ceilings also. There was a primitive cast iron range in the kitchen with a plain deal table and forums for seating. We were left some single iron bedsteads, military style blankets, hard pillows and strong mattresses. A fuel house, store house, some turf and some coal was left in this structure and a dry type lavatory was attached.

On a cold winter's evening I assembled our armed party at the entrance to the town of Abbeyfeale, twelve in number including Jack Aherne and Batt Wrenn, both lately released from prison, Tom Boucher, battalion police officer, Jack McAuliffe, late R.I.C., Larry and Johnny Harnett, Jack Lynch, Dan Cullinane, Denis Collins, Jack Leahy, Paddy Aherne and myself. On being given the order "quick march", we tramped down through the main street to the apparent surprise of the citizens, passed through the main entrance gate to the barracks and each of us made a scramble to be first to get the most comfortable bed. Alas, they all looked cold and dreary in their drab setting, but such a damper on our spirits did not deter us from cooking our first meal and enjoying it in our new environment. Faced with the problem of cooking, we engaged a middle-aged woman by the name of Mary Barry to come each day at a small wage to do the cooking for us. At that time till the I.R.A. split in June 1922 the Army authorities allowed us a maintenance sum every month. From June onwards we had to depend on local shops for our sustenance till we evacuated the barracks in August. Poor old Mary Barry had her work cut out for her in the looking after and feeding of twelve hungry men, and keeping the place passably clean. She liked a sup of porter, preferably a frothy pint. This was a tough job, but neither Mary nor the "boys" were too particular. The lice followed us everywhere and soon found shelter in our new quarters. Porter was cheap then and many's the free pint some of the boys got from girl friends in some of the premises frequented by them. Many's the box of fags slipped into their pockets on the sly. Sometimes the proprietor of one of these friendly "bars" was a thirsty man himself and handed out some free drinks in a truly generous mood. He too accepted drinks from the "boys" unknowingly at his own expense. The girl friends camouflaged well all this flow of liquor in a truly bewildering manner. I watched this in amazement, but being at that time not partial to intoxicating drink, it had not the same appeal for me.

Our police officer, Tom Boucher, was kept busy during our time in the barracks. He had to implement the decisions of the Sinn Féin courts, both district and parish. The chairman of the Abbeyfeale court was Fr. Fitzgerald C.C., and he often imposed heavy fines for officers convicted. This did not make us popular in the district as some fines imposed bore no resemblance to reality. Our police were often most reluctant to carry out these verdicts of the Sinn Féin court in Abbeyfeale. During the early summer unpaid rates were collected by the rate collectors going round from door-to-door, assisted by the Volunteer police. Seizure of goods had to be made in some instances. These seizures were sometimes violently opposed by the people directly involved. Here the help of ex-policemen from the old R.I.C. was invaluable. I can assure you they were not loved, but their training in a hard school made them impervious to all insults. Maybe some people believed that under a native administration (rents and rates were a tax imposed by the British) they were now freed from paying.

In the town we had to maintain order, patrol the streets each day and night, see that order was kept and closing time was observed in the public houses. As some of our troops were thirsty men it was difficult to maintain discipline, especially on Fair days. Then the countryfolk insisted on treating them liberally to whiskey and Guinness, not that it took much persuasion.

We had to contend with a lot of people, men and women who poured out stories about underground co-operation between the Black and Tans and townspeople. Jealous young women too caused us a lot of annoyance, relating stories on the same theme. Under pressure from these unrealistic sources we were obliged to hold investigations into these allegations. I was in the invidious position of having to preside at our court of inquiry. It looks ridiculous now that such unimportant disputes between rival groups of young girls should have been seriously investigated by any man in his sane senses. I think the brainless co-operation by some I.R.A. men in backing a certain faction and all the efforts they made to blacken their opponents as enemy collaborators, without any real proof, were really vindictive acts. Without any doubt, there were allegations made about certain people in the town, as being rather too friendly with the Black and Tans.

On a few occasions Jimmy Collins and myself met by appointment a police constable by the name of Pattison, who was an Ulsterman serving in Abbeyfeale during the period that the police and Tans occupied the barracks there. He was friendly to our Sinn Féin movement and during our talks with him he never disclosed the names of anybody assisting the police. He did say though, that bottles of whiskey, brandy and eatables were slipped over the barrack wall at night, from people anxious to please them. On one occasion in 1920, he tipped off Jimmy Collins about it being known in the barracks that some of the column were to meet their girlfriends near the bridge spanning the river near Knockbrack. These girls, from time to time, came out during the evening and brought the most needed items in their bags to their boys and cigarettes were prominent on the list. Pattison's tip saved the boys from capture.

During the spring and early summer of this year, divisions began to appear in our Army. Some obeyed orders of the Provisional government and began to occupy many barracks and buildings in various towns and cities. Desperate efforts were made to heal these divisions, without success. A convention was held in Dublin between the divided sections of the Republican Army in late March and it was believed that the rift was healed.

Our brigade council, presided over by the Brigade Commandant, Garrett McAuliffe, selected two delegates to attend this convention, namely Con Foley, 3rd Battalion O/C, Broadford and Ben Sullivan, his Vice Commandant representing West Limerick's I.R.A. Prior to this brigade council, at a meeting attended by the brigade and five battalion staffs, we solemnly reiterated our pledge to defend the Irish Republic, as originally proclaimed on Easter Monday, 1916, and confirmed on the 21st day of January, 1919, by elected members of Dáil Éireann in the Mansion House, Dublin.

In our area of West Limerick, buildings were occupied by some officers and men of our brigade, who had transferred their allegiance to the Provisional government. It was a difficult time, trying to keep peace between our troops and the now openly called Free Staters or regular Irish Army, dressed in green overcoats, jackets, yellow gaiters, yellow boots and breeches. And to crown it all they were paid the then generous wage of twenty-five shillings per week and their keep. It had a staggering impact on poor, needy labourers and ex-British soldiers, all without money or work. So it was good-bye to Republicanism, which most did not understand anyway. Friction and armed attempts by our troops to attack and capture some of these Free State strongholds led to all but armed conflict even before the attack on the Four Courts. It was overcome in West Limerick without loss of life and what a tragedy could have been averted if common sense had prevailed elsewhere.

To aggravate things, members of the I.R.A. lately released from prison were not content or happy at the role that they now had to play in our ranks, as the positions vacated by them had been filled by others when they were captured. On their release they were out of things and left in a rather invidious position of being unattached pro-tem. They could certainly take their place in the ranks and serve the cause as humble

soldiers, which some just did, until a stable situation arose to
examine their status in the I.R.A. If they felt called upon or
impelled by desire for a military life in the country's service in
peace time, an opportunity might arise when they could do so.
But unfortunately, at the time I am writing about, nothing of
a satisfactory nature existed to show that we had ended the
war—supposedly the last fight ending long centuries of succes-
sive and seemingly endless oppression.

Early in the fateful year of 1922 our people were split
hopelessly asunder, a tragic forerunner of worse to come. This
was reflected in our area and in the towns of West Limerick—
as elsewhere in the country—as two distinct armed forces were
in occupation of different buildings. In June 1922, things looked
very serious, as open conflict seemed each day nearer.

One day I was visited by Brigade Officer Michael Keane,
who had command of the Free State forces in West Limerick.
He was accompanied by a Captain in that Army, a native of
East Limerick, and former member of the East Limerick Brigade
Flying Column. Keane invited me into Moloney's Hotel, and
we had refreshments. We also had an earnest discussion on
the existing military and political situation, followed by an
invitation to join the Free State Army, with the promise of the
rank of Commandant. I declined, and still gave my allegiance
to the Republic.

Amongst the I.R.A. remaining loyal to the Republic in
Abbeyfeale, it was heartbreaking for them to see each day
former comrades in the uniform of a force pledged to subvert
all that was dear to them, attempting to take over duties till
then performed by them so well. At that time no overt act
was permitted to cause friction between both forces, as all the
time attempts were being made to reunite and prevent open
conflict. In spite of peaceful efforts, hotheads in the I.R.A. made
isolated armed (sniping) attacks on them. One such attack was
made by a few members of our Republican Army occupying
the police barracks in Abbeyfeale on a garrison of the Free
State troops in the neighbouring Ellis Mansion in the dead
hours of the night. The garrison panicked and rushed pell mell

down to the basement, without firing a shot in their defence. I had to reprimand our men who carried out this attack. Two of them were released prisoners and the other suffered from the after-effects of a wound, received in the Anglo-Irish conflict. But I think Guinness played a part in their action.

Early in the summer of 1922 my wife came to reside with me at my home in Killaculleen. She drove in to Abbeyfeale at the week-ends in a pony and trap to bring me to spend a day, preferably Sunday, at home, and drove me back to our barracks on Monday. She got to know very well the Kelly girls, the neighbours and members of the Cumann na mBan in the town and district. As a nurse residing in a country parish, her services were often needed. Many a neighbour she nursed back to health and helped too at the dying bedsides of many in the district. The I.R.A. and Free Staters that also came her way as wounded men during the Civil War were attended with equal care.

In our barracks an uneasy restlessness afflicted us and standing idly by watching events which were beyond our control was hard on one and all. During fine spells we played games, handball especially, and had many a swim in a big pool in the nearby river Feale. In fact, some of us became proficient swimmers and divers. A brigade officer, Commandant Michael Colbert, was sent to our barracks as a restraining influence on any hasty actions by our men. But I must say he spent a lot of time drinking and paying courtship to two rival young ladies who entertained him, each in the confines of their parents' pub, as he switched his custom around.

Early in June circulars from Dublin were sent around to the president of each Sinn Féin cumann to be placed before the members. These circulars asked for a motion to be put to each cumann by the chairman asking for support for the Provisional government set up to implement the Treaty. In some cases these proposals were approved, as often the chairman of the cumann was the local Catholic curate who generally advocated acceptance of them. One priest was chairman of a parish cumann where there were two churches; he was the presiding officer at both meetings held after Mass. In one parish, where the farmers were comfortable, when asked for their views, voted for acceptance on his advice. In the other, a poorer district where the farms were small with a sprinkling of labourers, on being asked for their views voted to remain in the Sinn Féin organisation.

At that time we held parades in each company area of the I.R.A. in West Limerick. I asked them at each assembly to re-affirm their allegiance to the Republic and defend it with their lives. I well remember some who attended and joined in this loudly acclaimed renewal by each of their former pledge given when originally they had joined the Republican Army. Alas, only a few days afterwards some could be seen in the uniform of the Staters.

Around the period (27–28 June) of the attack on the Four Courts, Free State soldiers occupying the buildings in West Limerick withdrew to swell their forces in Limerick City. Before we were really seriously ready to combat our new foes, they had taken the initiative everywhere after capturing the Four Courts and other strong places in Dublin by 5 July. I thought then and still do, that we underestimated them and the public support they received. The newspapers of that day prepared the ground for their eventual success, by their propaganda and one-sided dissemination of news. Another thing, we never took seriously the action taken by the Provisional government and did not vigorously oppose it. Firstly it took us completely by surprise; secondly we did not seriously believe that they really meant it; and thirdly we were beaten without doing anything dramatic to prevent their offensive operations. All too true we were caught napping and our military potential wasted in a defensive campaign that lost us the initiative we should have grasped. It did not sink in for a long time, the tragic fact that our brothers-in-arms could be so ruthless and brutal. The truth is, our hearts were not in it, and this alone contributed a good deal to our military defeat.

It is rather ironic now to relate that the I.R.A. men of the rank and file seemed to grasp the realities of the situation as it emerged during the fighting in Dublin, and even prior to that event. In our discussion often it was regarded as strange that a new army was allowed to be created, recruited and armed without any effort being made to prevent its formation. It struck us as monstrous that our superior officers in the I.R.A. could countenance such a force that threatened the very existence of the Republic. Another thing that appealed very much to the Volunteers in the I.R.A.: why wait to be attacked piecemeal all over the country? It would be better by far if the Republican G.H.Q. staff organised columns of men from all areas to converge on Dublin with speed. Confine the battle to the City and drive the Free State soldiers off the streets, capture their artillery and turn it on themselves, arrest the members of the Provisional government and temporarily have military rule. There may be snags in this, one being British intervention, but far better to fight a war against them than to destroy one another.

In July, during the escalation of the fighting over the country, our staff discussed the shortage of transport we suffered from. So it was decided that I take some three armed men with me to commandeer some motor cars or trucks. So one fine Sunday in July we drove to Rathkeale where ex-British officers resided on estates in the town's vicinity. We drove into the drive, leading to a mansion occupied by a Major Longford. I knocked at his hall-door and on this gentleman appearing, I informed him that we were I.R.A. men commandeering cars and trucks for the use of our forces. There on his front drive was a valuable Maxwell motor car, with left hand driving wheel, the first I had ever seen. Despite his protests we put one of our men, Stephen Mulcaire, behind the wheel, and on finding no other vehicle, drove off in the Maxwell.

Next we invaded the grounds of the Protestant Church, where a service was taking place. It was not a nice thing to do, but at this time we thought that the Protestants were our enemies and on the side of the Free State. We waited until their service was ended and when the churchgoers came out to depart in various modes of transport, we halted those who sought to drive off in some half-dozen or so small motor cars. We told these people that we belonged to Michael Collins's men, then expected in Tralee from Fenit, from which port they invaded Kerry. Explaining that we had to secure cars to transport us there quickly as part of a Free State column ordered to join up with those coming by sea. Luckily for our sedate middle-aged Protestant churchgoers, the cars they owned were totally unsuitable for our purpose, being all two-seaters. So leaving the place disgusted, we raided several places from Rathkeale to the Shannon. We got nothing for our day's trouble, but nonetheless enjoyed our adventure over the fertile and lovely part of Limerick. We were the envy of our comrades returning in our smashing motor car. This car did a lot of work for us, and finally ended its days shortly afterwards, at the end of August, when necessity compelled us to destroy it.

Our brigade headquarters in Newcastle West was situated in the Castle, a fine mansion, once under the rule of the Earl of Desmond. Our troops occupied it after the Treaty was signed, and remained loyal to the Republic. Its maintenance party comprised men from all five West Limerick battalions and numbered around forty men with the officers of the brigade staff, including a training officer, Georgie Wallace. His business also included security which included the posting of sentries, issuing passwords, and orderly duties,. His sentries were strictly ordered to allow no one into the Castle grounds, without the password or identification, especially at night.

One night a sentry posted at the entrance to the Castle was a boy named J. Hayes, a very nervous type and not used to the handling of weapons. He took the orders of George Wallace regarding his duties very seriously. On this particular night he heard footsteps approaching his post in the tree-darkened avenue. As this person approached towards him he cried "halt", and without waiting for identification, in a nervous haste put his rifle to his shoulder, aimed at the approaching figure, pulled the trigger and shot him dead. This sad occurrence cast a gloom over us all, as the Volunteer officer killed was Dan McEnerney, a fine looking man, six feet tall, very handsome, a grand singer and entertainer. He was betrothed to a beautiful young girl living in Newcastle West, who was heart-broken at his tragic end. We censured George Wallace over this tragic affair, as he had put the fright of God into many immature Volunteers during his training of them. George was formerly a Sergeant Major in an Irish regiment, lately demobilised by the British, and the authoritarian methods he had learned in that army he strove to imitate in the Republican Army.

During the protracted fighting in Limerick City between the Free State force under the command of Mick Brennan and our Republicans, we sent a quota of our men to help the beleaguered garrison manning the Strand barracks, William Street barracks, the jail and strong places in the city. As the fighting developed in intensity with the advance of the Staters down through the country and our quick retreat before their greater strength and immensely greater firepower provided by their eighteen-pounder guns, our resistance collapsed. To this conventional type warfare, we had no answer. In Limerick we lost one of our West Limerick column men, Paddy Naughton, who was mortally wounded. He was shot by a sniper's bullet in an attempt to retrieve a can of condensed milk.

After the capture of Limerick our troops withdrew to Adare and then to Rathkeale and Newcastle West, closely pressed by the attacking Staters. Casualties were inflicted on us, as our men withdrew. At Adare Mrs. Hartney, a Cumann na mBan member and first aid worker, was killed by a rifle bullet. Her husband Captain Michael Hartney was a member of the Mid-Limerick Brigade and her death was a great shock to him and her friends. Our men defended Newcastle West for a whole day. During the fighting the Free Staters' big guns were trained on the Castle and it was demolished in a short time. Surrounding the town on all sides, our forces were compelled to fight their way out or be captured. In this withdrawal two Republicans lost their lives and sad to relate they were brothers.

Brigade Adjt. Jimmy Collins and some others failed to leave in time, and were trapped for several days before escaping to safety. Collins and some comrades were compelled to seek refuge in the old Courtney Arms Hotel as their retreat from the town was cut off. There they stayed in discomfort in the attic, assisted by a few maids working in the hotel till a favourable moment came to effect their escape. Creeping down the stairs in their bare feet, in the dead of night past sleepy half-drunk sentries, Jimmy Collins arrived at my house in Killaculleen the following night and thrilled us all with his vivid description of his stay in the attic and subsequent escape. On 4 August 1922 Newcastle West fell, and with it all resistance in the accepted sense of open warfare. We in our post in Abbeyfeale kept in touch with Newcastle during the fighting there, and after the defeat suffered by our forces, made preparations to evacuate our posts, burn them to the ground, and retreat to Newmarket, Co. Cork. Despite appeals from some of the townsfolk to spare some of the buildings, we reluctantly had to refuse their request, as the business of war is to make everything of value useless to the enemy, if possible.

Our sincere friends in the town lamented our quick departure and in the after days when the guns were silenced and deep hatreds were dying down, we could calmly discuss the tragic happenings of those terrible times and sometimes get a good laugh at incidents recalled. It amused me a lot at that time, the approach to me in the evening of our evacuation of Abbeyfeale by a young man of good appearance and pronounced American accent. He gave me his name and recounted at length his record and experience in the American Expeditionary Force to Europe during the Great War. He told me he was anxious to join the Republican Army and enquired where was the recruiting station situated, as he wanted to become a member of our army at once. On the night of our evacuation our headquarters was at a farmhouse. The yank, when he saw the place, disappeared during the night.

One day we lay in wait to ambush a party of Free State troops being conveyed by motor transport between two towns—chatting amongst ourselves regarding the consequence of what we were about to engage in. Some said they felt it extremely hard and difficult for them to fire a rifle shot to kill maybe some neighbour or fellow countryman. Right enough, when the "Staters" ran into our positions we fired our guns over their heads and to our complete surprise they surrendered in a few minutes. Their officers drove off like hell out of the place and left their men at our mercy.

We Republicans, I maintain, never fought this Civil War as a war ought to be fought. We found it hard to convince ourselves that our foes were deadly serious. Events convincingly proved their determination, and made their ruthlessness clear. My home in Killaculleen, for a time in August and September, was like a miniature hospital, as we treated some wounded men there, having received them in aforementioned attacks. My wife, being a trained nurse, had her hands full looking after them. We also had some Free State prisoners on parole and amongst them was a former hotel chef who catered to our needs. We had an assorted quantity, if not quality, of foodstuffs got in raids on the trains nearby. Between bouts of activity we lazed our days away and the weather being fine, things looked good. But ominous clouds were appearing, and we knew these days could not last. We then decided to get rid of our prisoners, poor Mac our chef included. I borrowed some money and clothes from a bank manager to provide them with something in their pockets, and civilian clothes instead of the uniforms they were dressed in. I bid them farewell and parted, never to meet again.

After the evacuation in West Limerick of all our buildings, we once again reverted to our old guerrilla tactics, and surprise attacks on enemy posts. When we withdrew from Abbeyfeale it was occupied by boys and men recruited from the neighbouring parishes of Brosna, Duagh, Knocknagoshel, Moyvane and Tarbert, all in Kerry. Their officers included Walter Broderick, lately an officer in the British Army, Jack Horgan and a few others. The force amounted to about fifty men, under the command of these officers. They occupied Mrs. Eccliston's Drapery establishment and W. D. O'Connor's premises attached to it. At the back was an enclosed yard having the shops on the street side where the officers resided. This building commanded the yard belonging to Ecclistons and O'Connors. As Ecclistons was a corner house at a street junction, it controlled approaches from the Square, leading to the Tralee road, the road to Listowel and the main street leading to Limerick. Across the yard from these shops was a two-storeyed strongly constructed building, with windows and doorway facing Ecclistons. There were billeted the Free Staters and petty officers. They put out patrols on all roads leading to the town, day and night, and posted sentries at regular intervals, and observed all military rules, as well as unseasoned troops could do.

At a council meeting convened at my home in Killaculleen, attended by Adjt. Jimmy Collins, Willie Flynn, battalion intelligence officer, Jerry Moloney and myself, we learned from Flynn the set-up of our opponents, and acted accordingly as follows: we planned to steal into the town in the early hours of a September morning, with parties of men about twelve in each under a reliable officer. Altogether we had four such groups. One was to come in by the Athea road, one from the Newcastle direction, one from Meenahela to come in over the fields and emerge on the main street, and lastly another was to enter by the Killarney road. All had definite instructions and were to arrive at a specified time for each party. Michael Colbert and Garrett McAuliffe led the troops from Athea, and slipped into the town without the patrols observing them. Their job was to slip into O'Connors and Ecclistons, assisted by a local I.R.A. man who secured entrance for them by getting possession of the keys from friendly girls working in these shops. They were to disarm and overpower the officers sleeping upstairs. The three other parties, at a signal from the advance party, were to rush from the houses nearby temporarily occupied by them, where after converging on the town they lay hidden.

The advance party successfully did their work and secured as prisoners in a rear room their discomforted opponents. After giving us a few minutes to emerge on the streets and join them in the houses and to occupy O'Connors's yard commanding the building in possession of the Free State troops,

firing started almost immediately. The party I was in crossed
the main street, and just as we did, who should appear from
around the corner of the Eccliston building but two soldiers
on patrol duty. They got such a fright on seeing us, that they
offered no resistance. We pushed them before us into a house
to be held prisoner during the fight. As Jimmy Collins, Sonny
Quaid, Jim Roche, Jack McAuliffe, P. J. O'Neill, Jerry Moloney
and the rest of our troops rushed to join our comrades, passing
by Mrs. Shanahan's we were, believe it or not, invited in for
a few quick drinks. Despite our urgency to join the fight, we
delayed long enough to sample a few glasses of malt. Rushing
out, we fired some quick rifle shots at houses across the street
where we were informed a couple of officers were billeted.
These never replied even by a single shot, but got away at the
back as we learned later.

At the double we rushed down the street, a short distance
from Mrs. Shanahan's to O'Connors' yard, where we took up
positions. We fired at the windows in the second storey building,
from which rifles were now discharging their deadly message
in all directions. As we ran down the street we saw men emerge
from the Killarney road and advance cautiously. When they
saw us they mistook our troops for Staters. It was amusing to
see them jump into doorways and archways when we advanced.
I recognised the foremost amongst them—Tim O'Connor—
and when he and his comrades pointed their guns in our
direction it was amusing no longer. Coming to a halt I called
out to them who we were, and as they advanced, placed their
force in a position to cover the main double doors giving
access to the road from the enclosed yard and the building
where the Staters were now trapped.

Shortly after this, Danny Lane, Tommy Leahy and others
from this fourth party arrived. A heavy line of fire was now
concentrated on the troops trapped in the building. To frighten
them more, Sonny Quaid got a ladder, placed it against the
gable, mounted it and commenced to break the slates on the
roof and started to pour petrol into the interior. This caused
the defence to collapse, though in any event they had none,

as the place was untenable. Its windows were not protected by
sandbags or defensive material. In fact the glass of these were
deadly weapons also, and caused some wounds amongst the
garrison. Having no officers to direct their defence, they lost
heart from the evidence of seeing a dozen or so of their
comrades wounded, a few seriously and certain death awaited
some, if battle continued. Then someone hung out a white
flag and it was all over after a period of deafening rifle fire and
ribald shouts by our troops.

It was a quick collapse and I can assure you our foes, after
that baptism of fire, were very tame young men. Dr. Eddie
Harnett, my cousin and our medical officer, was summoned
to the battleground where he gave medical attention to the
wounded. Lining our dejected enemies before us in this barrack
yard, lately controlled by them, it was hard to realise the stark
reality of such a situation. Here was arrayed a body of young
men, lately our friends and fellow soldiers, serving the same
cause, now so utterly opposed to it. I believe, for hungry men,
twenty-five shillings a week, a fine uniform, houses, and the
best diet that they had ever had, made it easy to get recruits
and willing slavish obedience in pursuit of a policy, practically
of shoot first and damn the consequences.

When the fight was over, some thirty souls had their fill of
whiskey and Guinness. J. Woulfe got real mad, and with a
rifle in his hand threatened to shoot our Brigade O/C and
had to be forceably disarmed before he carried out his threat.
He meant it too, as a short time before, he was up before
a military court presided over by our Brigadier, just before
we lost our barracks. He was sentenced to be confined to a
restricted area for a period of a few weeks, and deprived of
certain privileges.

We stripped the Free State barracks of all its material, rifles,
beds, bedding, ammunition, cooking utensils, stores and
uniforms. Mustering the fifty or so men and officers captured
into some kind of formation, we marched them along the
main Newcastle road with their baggage on some farm carts,
bringing up the rear. Arriving at Devon Road cross we halted,

as I was not sure what to do with our prisoners, who in any event would surely make a bee-line for the nearest garrison town. Whilst we halted there, one of the captured officers, Lieut. J. Horgan, got very noisy and mouthed some filthy remarks about Mick Mahony, one of the guard escort. Mick pulled back the bolt of his rifle and shoved a bullet in the breech, put it up to Lieut. Horgan's head and pulled the trigger. Standing beside him, I instinctively struck his rifle with a blow of my hand and the bullet passed quite close to Lieut. Horgan's head. After this incident I decided to let the prisoners free, and after marching them for a further couple of miles up a byroad did so. Shortly after this day's work, all our prisoners again rejoined. Some were sent to East Limerick to serve and there J. Horgan was accidentally killed in a motor crash.

After our successful fight in Abbeyfeale, Column Commander Michael Colbert, with a party of our men, attacked Tarbert barracks on a Sunday morning. He was assisted by some of the Kerrymen in the locality. They were helped by the intelligence that they obtained about the number of Free State troops in occupation there and their habits on Sundays. It was planned to attack during early Mass in the parish church, situated in the town. A party of troops marched there to Mass, half for first Mass. The other half attended late Mass from the barracks with their officers. Thus, it meant for our troops that if the Staters attending early Mass were prevented from leaving the church during the attack on those remaining in the barracks, it would deprive the garrison of much needed help. It worked out as planned. Michael Colbert personally saw to the investment of the church, and saw the parish priest, Fr. J. O'Connor (who was a first cousin of my wife). Explaining to Fr. O'Connor that it was important that none of the soldiers leave the church and that this order applied to all parishioners, including himself, the parish priest got into a great rage, but it was futile as was his condemnation of the I.R.A., when he spoke to his congregation during Mass.

Our men moved quickly down towards the barracks by the fields and gardens, and entered houses facing the old police station and adjoining buildings beside it, quietly from the back. The Staters had no protection from attack, as the windows in their barracks were not protected by sand-bags or defensive material. They were taken completely by surprise, and finally, when a successful attempt was made by our men to set it on fire, they gave up, after putting up a stiff resistance. They suffered the same disaster as did the Abbeyfeale garrison and lost approximately the same number of men, guns, ammunition and stores. But it was only a temporary setback for them as, in a few days, they again were armed and in occupation of the same building. After the aforementioned attacks on the Staters, we dispersed into small groups in our own areas. It was the beginning of the end for us as an effective force, and spelled the end of organised attacks on our foes.

I went home during September, and helped with the last of the haymaking that year. One day as I was in our big meadow, saving hay with my father and a few others, we saw coming along the road from Abbeyfeale a large armed column of Free State troops. They passed by our meadow, but did not halt or approach us, or the house to make searches. I felt I was very lucky that they did not stop or attempt to approach us. Years later I met the officer of that column in O'Connell Street, Dublin, and had a chat with him. He informed me that he recognised me that day in 1922, but kept the news to himself. So, thanks to an honourable foe, I had some extra days of liberty.

Shortly afterwards, the Free State Army chiefs made a change in the disposition of their forces and this played a big part in our defeat, though at that time in September we had lost the war. This change was the removal from their own areas of the men recruited into their army, and transfer to other areas. This meant the removal of men, one time intimate friends of ours and probably reluctantly opposed to former comrades now. In a good many cases their conscience would not allow acceptance of the ruthless methods advocated and carried out against neighbours. Though this may be true I can assure you that some had no such thing as a conscience. Some of our men were even forced into callous indifference by events. Henceforth in West Limerick till the end the garrisons in all our towns were men from the 1st Western Division, principally from Galway and East Limerick. Their officers were a mixture of West of Ireland, East Limerick and one Kerryman. Mixed through these strangers was a sprinkle of local men, who knew the people in each area. These were necessary as otherwise it would be difficult to identify I.R.A. men. Some local Free State soldiers were not much better than spies; most objectionable was the behaviour they showed in searches of neighbours' houses.

At this time searches became frequent and in a couple of weeks the Free Staters had, in wide encircling sweeps of districts, caught a surprising number of our men. Now, instead of making offensive raids, the men were engaged in trying to escape from the net. Hundreds of troops were out day and night searching the country, and even if we had stayed together in columns to resist them we would have failed. The element of surprise was now lost by us, and also the support we once had from the bulk of the people. At my home in Killaculleen we still had some wounded men and prisoners. These were released as we could do nothing else, as our own position deteriorated from day to day.

One evening near the end of September, some dozen or so men of our column were gathered for the last time, never to meet again as such. This gathering took place at my home in Killaculleen and included Commandant Tadg Crowley, Ballylanders, Dick Longford, Jack Aherne, Jerry Moloney, Paddy Aherne, Denis Collins, Larry Harnett, Liam Callaghan, Martin Ward, Jack McAuliffe, Jack Leahy, and Jimmy Collins, Brigade Adjt. From this evening onwards, no determined attempts were made to mount armed attacks against the Staters, except sniping at them from a distance.

CHAPTER VII.

A GUEST OF THE NATION, 1922–1923.

Being at my home for a few days helping with the haymaking, it did not penetrate into my mind that it was now becoming really dangerous, even during the daytime, to remain at home. And so it happened. One evening as I was doing some carpentry in an outhouse, I came out into the yard and before I realized what was happening the whole place was overrun with soldiers. In charge of them was Commandant Fallon, and Captain Glynn from the Western Division. Commandant Fallon, with a gun stuck to my head, threatened to shoot me out of hand if I made any move to get away. As I tried to enter the house to see my wife, he prevented me from doing so, until she came out to ask that I be at least allowed to enter, to put together an extra shirt, socks and shaving outfit. As we stood there arguing our servant girl rushed into the yard, much out of breath from running from the village about a mile away, to warn me that the Free State troops were drinking in the pubs there. Unfortunately they beat her in the race and so apprehended me. Poor Mag, as a result was in tears and whispered to me that in a certain house the Staters were tipped off as to my whereabouts that evening. So, bidding a sorrowful farewell to my wife, relatives and Mag, I marched up our long boreen to the road in the dusk of the evening.

Captain Glynn stuck by my side all that night and it being a moonlight one, I had no chance of escaping. After capturing me, they marched back again to the village and afterwards in a straggling column we moved to the town of Newcastle West.

We did not hurry at any speed, but made a few searches of suspect houses en route. At one house we stopped for some time and the inmates to me seemed to be friendly with the officers. In fact one of them came out to identify me as the troops did not seem sure who I was until this identification. We finally arrived at the police barracks, situated in the town square. I was the only Republican brought in by the raiding party that morning, and only one other prisoner was there before me stretched on a pile of dirty Army blankets. He was known to me as Dan Collins, a brother of our Sinn Féin T.D. Con Collins, both from Monegae.

Some of our guards doing duty in the barracks were from the town, and one of these was Jimmy Hannon (a brother-in-law of Sean Moylan, O/C North Cork I.R.A.). He was helpful and offered me some whiskey to drink. This I declined with some rudeness as at this time I felt sorry for myself and took it out on Jimmy. Shortly afterwards we got some tea, food, bread and butter served up in a primitive fashion. From that day onwards, until I was released, food and cigarettes were topics of conversation and came up regularly in our chats, as I can assure you we never got enough to fill our healthy stomachs except on rare events. As I looked out the window when this repast was over, a large body of men marched into the square from Castlemahon and Clouncagh districts surrounded by troops. In double ranks they were lined up, facing the window out of which I was gazing, and I knew some of them. A couple of officers went along the ranks questioning each man in turn. I was amazed at seeing some I knew well being asked to leave the ranks and told there and then they were released. The others were kept in their ranks for some time, then Dan Collins and myself were brought to join them. Some armed guards belonging to the 1st Western Division surrounded us on both sides and headed by their officers, we were marched up the street to the railway station, to entrain for Limerick and then imprisonment in the jail there.

I remember well the filthy conditions of the cells, and corridors, the smell from the filthy lavatories, always in a dirty condition from urine and filth. One landing after another was surrounded by iron mesh railings; in the vicinity of the toilets (with only a couple, one at each end to serve each landing), urine was continually floating around their vicinity. This was carried into the cells on the boots of prisoners, who were packed, eight men into each at night, lying side by side on dirty mattresses and army blankets on the cell floor. At the back was the exercise yard surrounded by high walls and watch towers at each corner, manned by armed sentries. These walls held arc lamps at night, and these lights lit up the walls and yard. At the farthest end from the prison was a toilet, beside one of these high walls, and it was in a position for public gaze, for it was exposed for all to see. In the confines of the prison the lice thrived and made our life hell, day and night.

Nothing surprised me as much as to see all the captured boys and men from West Limerick, whose fate was similar to my own. It looked as if the Free State troops must have worked fast and successfully in our area to capture in their net most of our fighting men in a short time. The rest outside must be hunted and harried from place to place, now that the war had our boys driven relentlessly by a ruthless foe into a primitive existence. We were, I think, carelessly checked by the prison officers on our admittance to Limerick prison, and our identities were mostly unknown. I was not long there when I heard of an attempted escape one night over the high wall with the aid of a plank of wood. This plank was to cross over a wide passageway between the prison wall and the high boundary wall of the asylum nearby. Some of the boys making this escape attempt pushed out the plank from the prison side to cross over to join the wall of the asylum. But it failed to connect, being somewhat short. During this attempt one prisoner slipped off the plank and fell into the passage-way. He remained there till morning when he slipped in through the main doorway, as the milk was being delivered. Some commotion was made as well as some noise, in the attempt to escape, and the sentries, when they were alerted, opened fire. Luckily, no one was injured in the attempt. I learned all about it from Michael Colbert, one of the organisers and leaders of the party.

In the confusion created in Limerick jail by all the prisoners there, the prison officers found it difficult to establish any man's identity. I remember one gloomy evening we were surprised to see an officer and a party of troops march into our main corridor on the ground floor. Then lining the soldiers with rifles and fixed bayonets at one end of this corridor, their officer, with the aid of the military police, routed all of us out of the cells into a dense mass on the floor. The officer produced a paper and read out the names of some amongst us, asking them to step forward for identification. His request was met by a stony silence on our part, which infuriated him. He once again called out the names of those wanted, but to no avail. Then he issued an ultimatum to us: that if his request was not granted he would order his soldiers to open fire on us, and hold us responsible for the result. He in fact ordered the soldiers to get ready to shoot and at that moment one of our men, Sean Hynes, stepped forward and requested that we be allowed to recite a decade of the Rosary. Before any move was made or time given to the military, we all fell on our knees, and Sean Hynes led us to say this prayer. Our determination to resist at all costs won our battle. We were excommunicated Republicans, reviled by authority, lay and clerical, but triumphant in adversity.

I was not held in Limerick Jail very long; in fact, less than a week, and never was inside the prison chapel to attend Mass. During my short stay there, I was very intimate with Jimmy Collins, our Brigade Adjutant. He informed me that he intended to escape, and had worked out a novel plan to do so, the details of which he disclosed to me. Dan Collins had already applied for his release, and had signed a form repudiating his allegiance to the Republican Army and promising to obey the laws of the Free State. He was impatiently awaiting his release order. We were to persuade Dan to hand over his release form to our mutual comrade, Jimmy Collins. Jimmy was to answer to the name of Dan Collins, march up to the office and present his form as requested, and walk out a free man. Everything of course would be fine if Dan agreed, and really that was half the battle; the other half depended on not being recognised. We spent a few trying minutes persuading Dan to agree, especially the period after his name was called for release. By sheer luck we succeeded, though those trying moments were like hours. For Jimmy Collins, luck held, and he coolly marched out of the jail gates a free man. This was his second escape from his captors and yet once again when captured after some months' freedom, he on a third escape bid succeeded in getting free and was never again captured. Poor Dan Collins was very irritable and dissatisfied until the intercession of his brother Con Collins, T.D., opened the gates for him.

Early one morning we were assembled in the prison yard and we were informed that some were to be transferred to the Curragh in Kildare or elsewhere. Everyone was anxious to leave the dirty place, so on that morning there was no hesitation in answering the roll call. It was a cold frosty morning and when we appeared on the streets, we were surrounded on both sides by armed soldiers, acting as our guards. Some civilians appeared on the pavements and these cheered us loudly when we passed them by. We looked a ragged mob, as our clothes were unkempt as any you would find on a tinker's back. The Limerick people were not allowed near us, as on previous removals of prisoners they had fraternised with our boys, and in ejecting them, some prisoners quietly got away, as the soldiers did not know one from another. It did not happen on the morning I was removed. We arrived at the railway station and entrained for the Curragh, believing it to be our destination. We remained in ignorance until dark that night, when we arrived at Dublin's Kingsbridge Railway Station.

Lined up on the platform, surrounded by troops, we turned right around the station and marched up the road to Kilmainham. Nothing astonished me more than to see British soldiers entering and leaving a large barracks across the Liffey, as we marched along in a very disarrayed column. After a journey of half-a-mile or so, we arrived before the gates of that gloomy Irish Bastille—Kilmainham Jail. We were hustled inside and our force was divided up into parties of half-a-dozen or so into each cell with stone floors and they were ice cold. Besides being half-frozen, we were starved, being without food since early morning. Mugs of tea and a junk of bread were given to each prisoner by wardens. Gas jets faintly illuminated the ghastly place and as no beds or mattresses were given to us, we laid down to rest on our overcoats, on the flagged floor. It was, I remember, the most uncomfortable night I ever spent in prison. The cell I occupied in Kilmainham, with Jim Colbert, Willie Flynn, Mick Collins and some others, was that occupied by Dr. Kathleen Lynn, who was imprisoned there during Easter Week 1916. Her name was printed in large black letters on one of the interior walls of the cell. My companions and myself spent only one unforgettable night in this place.

After a tough night and day in Kilmainham we were transported in large trucks to Mountjoy Jail around the small hours of the following morning. Through a silent city we drove, without a human being in sight anywhere. It was a weird experience for us country lads and young men, but our morale was good despite our first taste of real hardship. Arriving in the prison yard of Mountjoy we came down off our lorries and lined up before the prison entrance. Here we were interrogated in what seemed a friendly manner by the Military Governor, Captain Phil Cosgrave. Some thought the signs looked good; his manner and behaviour was that of a gentleman. Alas, it was a delusion of a temporary nature as we soon discovered when we were ordered inside. Brought inside in groups of six men, we were placed standing before a large table, where we were interrogated by some officers seated behind it. They questioned each of us, relieved us of any cash we had, or watches, papers and documents.

Standing beside Jim Colbert I expressed indignation at their conduct in the treatment being meted out to fellow Irishmen in the conflict then raging. I was lucky to escape a beating as they ignored me completely. Not so lucky were others, notably

Georgie Wallace and Danny Corcoran. The military police (red caps) took great pleasure in giving them some resounding kicks on their backsides, as they conveyed them to the spiral stairway leading to a higher landing and so into their cells. It made us all feel like very small boys, when on entering our cells, we were ordered to take off our boots and socks for inspection and as well as that our clothes were searched. Jim Colbert looked at me, and in such a way he had when confronted with a situation out of the ordinary. He had a habit of pinching his ears and nose and sniffling to show his feelings.

The following morning we received a miserable, small portion of oatmeal porridge, a mug of terrible tea, some stinking butter and a small prison loaf. In our cell, Jim Colbert, Willie Flynn, Mick Collins and myself were accommodated in its small space. Our beds consisted of a single mattress, three grey blankets, two sheets for each prisoner. No pillows were provided so we made our boots covered by our overcoats as a substitute. Our beds were on the floor, laid side by side and took up all the floor space. We were given a couple of chamber pots for use at night, as nobody was allowed to leave their cells to go to the lavatory. We used one of our pots for cooking purposes at suppertime, to heat in it any spare stringy meat, cabbage, or spuds we did not eat at dinner. In fact you could get bits of gravel often in the cabbage and its gritty taste was most disagreeable. Over our gas jet we held our cooking pot until it heated sufficiently to eat its contents. Our worst diet was the rancid butter, which one smelled with disgust.

Prison experience is a hard education for anyone; but to suffer in prison as victims of Civil War, as we did, had its terrible humiliations, since we suffered at the hands of our fellow countrymen. I think it caused a sadistic tendency amongst the soldiers guarding their own kith and kin. Some of the officers and men engaged in this work seemed to my mind to be, in their dealings with the prisoners, absolutely dominated by some sinister force; exposing the dormant evil that lies hidden in a lot of people. Despite the restrictions of prison and internment, our Irish character of proven courage, humour and sadness never abandoned us, and hope of better times to come went a long way to assuage present sorrows. Spirits amongst us, whom nothing could subdue, were ever ready with some witty remark or story to cheer up the downhearted.

Deprived of parcels of food, cigarettes, letters or news-papers, we were cut off from the outside. Since our activity in Mountjoy was necessarily restricted, we did the best we could to pass the time each day in a somewhat orderly fashion. Our companions in adversity spent their waking hours visiting friends in the cells for chats, debates, studying the Irish lan-guage, reading and exercise in the yard. As one passed out from our wing to descend some steps leading to it, you passed by the execution chamber. It was of special interest, because of the I.R.A. men who suffered death there.

We received a great shock early in the month of December. It was the news that Rory O'Connor, Liam Mellows, Joe McKelvey and Dick Barrett were executed by firing squad in the early hours of the morning, it being the 8th day of December. These men were prisoners for a long time; they had been there since the previous June, when the Four Courts was destroyed. It filled us with black hatred of our captors and outraged our sense of justice. It made a mockery of law and the so-called establishment, that could commit legal murder, and put the Church into the position of trying to defend the thesis 'when is murder not a murder'.

Attending Mass on Sundays in the prison chapel was an ordeal, owing to the strictures we were under. It was a dreary place, where it was difficult to feel devout, surrounded by armed "red caps" as guards. Our chaplain, Canon Walters, was no friend of ours. His sermons were on topics far removed from the grim surroundings in which we listened inattentively to him. One of our comrades, William Colbert, was a very talented person. He was a first class black and white artist and drew the features and dress of some comical characters amongst us true to life. We often had a good laugh on viewing his pictures and I can still remember these sketches as if it were yesterday. Thanks to the artists amongst us, we were able at Christmas, 1922, to erect a temporary stage for the acting of a variety programme. This was much enjoyed and took place on the ground floor of our prison wing No. 4. The gloomy surroundings, on that night at least, were almost forgotten.

My companions and I spent three tough months in Mountjoy, where our other deadly enemies, the lice, took a hand in assisting the soldiers to torment us. During the winter months there, we did not feel the cold weather too badly, as a hot water pipe provided us at night with a fair amount of heat. The prison seemed, some nights, to be under severe bombardment by rifle fire and the din was terrific. It was customary for the sentries inside and outside to discharge their guns through the cell windows and along the four landings, usually at night. This was to deter any attempt to escape, so it was foolhardy to poke one's head out the open cell doors at night. During this firing, one evening I was just stepping down from having a peep through our small window, when, bang went a gun, as a rifle bullet passed through and struck the wall opposite and ricocheted off it, to be flattened against the side wall.

After three months of hardship, we were routed out one morning onto the ground floor, and there we were counted, handcuffed in pairs and our names taken. Without time to bid good-bye to our companions left behind, a couple of hundred of us were marched down the North Circular Road, to Kingsbridge Railway Station. There we were packed into compartments, like animals, in a train awaiting our arrival. In each compartment, open from one end of the railway carriage to the other, we were seated in pairs. Our guards stood with loaded weapons at either end, alert and ready to deal with us if the occasion arose. Then we departed, en route to the Curragh for internment.

The Curragh is about thirty miles from Dublin, and in a reasonably fast train can be reached in about forty minutes. Imagine our astonishment at the slow crawling way our train took to reach our destination. Between stops, moving into sidings and other frustrations it took us hours to reach the siding serving the Curragh camp. On our way we were not allowed to leave our seats, not even for an urgent demand of nature.

On our arrival at the Curragh "Tintown No. 2" our identities were established. Separated into large groups, we were put into corrugated roofed sheds, large enough to house about 100 men. The hut where I was housed had a rough concrete floor with beds ranged down each side with a very wide laneway between them. The walls too were corrugated and the windows, roof and walls were lined with felt. The corrugated iron walls did not quite reach the roof, which was supported by pillars. This left a space of about six inches along both sides at the top, with the wind blowing through. In January and spring it made for freezing conditions in our quarters. We had two cast-iron stoves centred apart in the middle to heat the place. At night when these were unattended it got very cold and so did we, so we devised a plan to conserve heat in our beds at night. These beds were single iron ones with spring mattresses, three grey army blankets, a hard pillow and two sheets, the latter never changed during the several months I spent there. To help to keep out the cold at night we tied both ends of our lower sheets to the head and bottom ends of our beds, making it into a hammock, next we packed on top of the bedclothes our overcoats and everyday apparel. Once in bed we pulled closer around us our hammock and by this means kept out a good deal of the winter cold.

The whole camp was surrounded by a barricade of barbed wire entanglements. The place was illuminated at night by huge lamps (electric), placed along the wire with the lights deflected downwards and inwards which made it as bright as daytime. Sentry boxes were placed at strategic points to control the prisoners from approaching near it and to prevent escape.

During my stay there two men escaped, getting out somehow through the main entrance. On the morning of their successful get-away I was speaking to one of them, Jim Sullivan. I could hardly believe my ears when he casually informed me that he was making an attempt in a short time. He had it all planned in detail with a van driver who was a daily visitor to the stores and was well known. This escape was successful and we were treated roughly after it by our jailors, as a reprisal.

Our camp was laid out on a bleak plain with rows of numbered huts facing each other like a street. Down below the huts was a primitive system of shelters for washing with little hot water at any time. Nearby were the toilet shelters in a row, made of corrugated zinc. Each structure was built over large buckets and open in front to the winds of heaven. A platform of rough boards surrounded the buckets and on the boards one crouched when nature demanded.

When we arrived at the Curragh in January we had to appoint our own officers to negotiate with the Free State Army men in control. Without this system it would have been impossible to run the camp efficiently in some ordered fashion, though often difficult. We had a good-sized compound to play games in and to indulge in sports from walking to running. Near the entrance gate was an office where everything coming in or out was checked. Our cook-house was nearby and we were allowed to have our men engage in preparing our meals. Beside this was our dining room and each day we had to pass by the counter of the cookhouse where our rations were doled out to us. Then we passed into the dining room and on rough deal tables placed our meals, which we ate standing up.

After getting the feel of the camp and my own hut, I quickly got to know all of my companions: where they came from, the circumstances of their capture and the parts played by them in recent events. A Dubliner, Peter White, a small young man, was elected as officer in our hut No. 12. His record in the fighting was well known as was the record of Christy Byrne, elected camp commdt. The commdt. had a staff, including medical doctors, and each hut had its personal officer. All these attended the meeting of the council regularly, heard complaints of every kind, from beatings by our guards to adverse treatment of prisoners during illness.

Disease struck us during spring, and many suffered chest ailments; some got pneumonia. One fine young man, Commandant Owen O'Brien from Castleconnell, developed pneumonia and died in our inadequate hospital. He was a grand man, kindly, of fine physique, over six feet tall, with a wonderful head of golden curls. He was an inmate of my hut and his untimely death was lamented by all who knew him. As a result of widespread illness embracing all the inmates our medical staff carried out an inspection of all underwear that we wore. Some they confiscated and burned in large incinerators. When the weather was starting to get warm the lice spread all over the ground in the vicinity of the toilets and made life a misery for us in bed and out of it. Alarmed at last by the danger of a virulent disease spreading, we had ourselves, our clothes and bed clothes fumigated in a huge disinfecting bath-house attached to the military barracks.

Those of us anxious to learn the Irish language got the use of a vacant hut and there for some hours each day, taught by Sean Kavanagh, the famous "Seán á Chota", we made good progress. When we left the Curragh we were well able to converse in Irish. "Seán á Chota" was a real character and a fluent native speaker. He was in America for a number of years and used to entertain us at each lesson as he reminisced, recalling his travels. One of the desires of his life was a love of porter; his glowing description of its dark frothy appeal for him was a lesson in itself. "No woman", Sean would say, "can ever take the place in my heart that I have for my dark pint."

Thoughts of escape were constantly in our minds, either by hunger strike or by tunnel under the wire surrounding our compound. We were all ordered to go on hunger strike and this order was to be carried out as a huge protest by over fifteen thousand men scattered in camps and jails all over the country. Whoever thought up this idea, that a massive protest undertaken by all prisoners would achieve success, made a bad mistake.

Considering all the types of men and boys interned—some with high ideals, others roped in during various searches, without the stamina or will to last through a long hunger strike—it was certainly going to be a failure, and it was. In my camp, as far as the bulk of the prisoners were concerned, it was over in twelve days. Some forty prisoners, imbued with the righteous thought of no compromise or surrender on the fundamental principle of Republicanism, carried on the hunger strike for a month or more, one dying in the process, before giving up. Depending on public support at that time was out of the question as a hostile press and propaganda rained down malediction on the "die hards", as we were then called.

In Tintown No. 1 camp, shortly after this, a tunnel was successfully bored through the deep sandy soil and an outlet made outside the barbed wire enclosing the camp. Over ninety prisoners escaped before their absence was discovered. Dan Bourke, later T.D. for Limerick and Lord Mayor of that city, was apprehended as he poked his head out of the tunnel. Asked where he was going, Dan replied as cool as you like, "Where am I going? I am going home." Alas, it was not to be for Dan the day of his deliverance from bondage.

My great friend Jim Colbert and Liam O'Callaghan made off together in the direction of Dublin. Arriving one night on Athgoe hill, on the Dublin/Kildare border near where the Liberator Dan O'Connell fought his famous duel with D'Esterre, they took shelter in an abandoned house. In the morning they espied below them a farmhouse a few hundred yards away. In desperation from hunger they cautiously approached and were welcomed by its inmates and provided with food and a bed to lie on. The owner of this house, Dick Smith, a Wicklow man and a friend of mine in later years, arranged to make contact with a friend of his in charge of a barge on the Grand Canal, plying between Dublin and Limerick. So at night they crept cautiously down the fields, guided by Dick Smith, who introduced them to the bargeman. There in the interior of this boat they hid and reached the outskirts of Limerick, despite the fact that military, on a couple of occasions, questioned the bargeman but never searched the vessel.

The aftermath of this escape had severe repercussions for us in our camp No. 2. The immediate result was a drastic search of our huts during the progress of which we were herded by soldiers, like sheep, to the farthest end of our compound and kept there for several hours. Unfortunately, in one hut evidence of an attempt to escape was discovered at the end of the building, where behind the boarding was found an entrance to a tunnel. The entrance was behind one of the beds and camouflaged by pictures, books and shelves. Life for us was a hell on earth for some time afterwards. The immediate result was that we were compelled to dig a deep trench along the inside of the barbed wire enclosure so that tunnelling would be of no use to facilitate escape.

On the first morning that the soldiers invaded our huts, their officer called the names of about thirty men and ordered them to line up outside. I was fortunate that morning that I escaped the ordeal of those ordered outside. The men, now standing at attention, were confronted by the O/C., Capt. Boylan. Facing them was a squad of armed soldiers with bayonets stuck on their guns. This officer addressed the prisoners and told them in no uncertain words that each day from now forward they would have to dig a trench so many feet deep until the whole compound was encircled by it. Spades, picks and shovels were brought for this purpose. Now came the real test as all the prisoners defiantly refused to pick up these implements and start digging. On the right hand of the line of prisoners was Tony Stack, Duagh, Co. Kerry; next was Sean Healy, North Cork.

The soldiers, on the order of this officer, advanced on the prisoners and, starting at the right with bayonets extended, started to prod Tony Stack. They menaced him dangerously, cutting his clothes front and back and wounding him. Despite this he still refused to budge. Moving on next to Sean Healy, the soldiers were about to continue this bayonet sticking down the line. Realising that someone might be killed, Stack consulted with Sean Healy in a whisper as to what should be done. Realising that defenceless men had no chance against the ferocious brutality of the soldiers and their sadistic officer, they gave in and we started weary months of digging under the supervision of this hated Capt. Boylan, backed up by lines of armed soldiers. I hated his guts as he arrogantly strutted around in abusive manner swinging his cane. He strode along on the brink of the trench over us and many a curse was placed on his fiery red head.

In our camp we had men from the four Provinces—amongst them native speakers from the Gaeltacht areas. The hut I was domiciled in had some talented men: Joseph Campbell of Laccandara, Co. Wicklow, poet and writer; Seán Ó Tuama, Gaelic speaker of Cork City; Seán Mooney, Vice-O/C., Dublin Brigade; Peter White, also a talented person (our hut officer); James White, later a higher executive officer; Dr. Liam Shortis, Ballybunion. We also had a veteran Battalion Commdt., P. J. Ryan, Dublin Brigade, one-time cowboy in western America and boxer, trained by the great John L. Sullivan himself. Spread through the camp were several more men talented in various ways and prominent in the I.R.A.

Our relationships with the Free State officers and personnel were never cordial. We often suffered at their hands at their indifference to our various problems; never would any of them address our camp staff by their military titles. Our hut O/C. was addressed as hut leader; likewise the same title was used in speaking to the camp O/C. We often had surprise searches of our huts, apart from the morning and evening roll calls. Prisoners being sought and badly required for some reason or another by the guards never had their identity revealed by anyone. God help anyone who clashed with the military police or Free State Commandant. The Free State Governor of our Tintown No. 2 camp was Commdt. McCormac. He inspected our huts frequently, accompanied by subordinate officers.

One of the most dangerous places in any hut was beside the entrance door with the occupants of the beds just inside (at either side). They nearly always bore the brunt of the brutal attacks launched against us from time to time. I well remember two young men from the West—after some fruitless search of our hut looking for incriminating documents—being brutally assaulted. They were dragged along the ground, pulled by their feet, with their heads bumping off the rough ground, until reaching the "Glasshouse", a place of terror where all classes of devices were applied to the unfortunate prisoner to cause suffering to his soul and body.

Surprise searches of the belongings of prisoners were frequent and we had to stand to attention at the foot of our beds. On one occasion a prominent prisoner in my hut had a lot of documents secreted in his bed. These related to affairs of interest to Republicans outside, mainly about our morale, our desire to escape and our future in the I.R.A., also the behaviour of our guards. Knowing that his bed and belongings would be searched he dumped the lot in my bed thereby making me an accessory if these documents were discovered in my possession. His action took me by surprise and hiding them as swiftly as possible I awaited the entrance of our searchers in a bad frame of mind. Immediately on their entrance and making straight for the bed of the prominent prisoner they ripped it apart, got nothing and then began searching several beds at random. Approaching my bed, they passed it by while all around me were beds in disarray, their belongings scattered on the floor.

The non-commissioned officer, known as "Socks", on his morning rounds of count and inspection was a typical soldier of the British Army. He was most insulting, aggressive and a dangerous person to clash with. One morning following one of many ugly incidents, as he stepped in through the big doorway with the privates following, he shouted "I am the camp commdt. and this is the hut leader." Pulling a Webley revolver from his holster he discharged a shot from it down over the men, still sleeping or lying on their bunks. Unfortunately he badly wounded one of us, a rather delicate person, lying on a bed just four bunks from me.

Apart from our digging operations, we spent a good deal of time occupied in making silver rings, Claddagh and other designs. We became experts in knitting scarves, making trousers out of brown blankets—cleaned our few shirts, socks and handkerchiefs. Some prisoners were really skilled at the work they did and the articles finished by them were a pleasure to look at. Decorations made in that camp lasted many a long year. I myself had a brown and yellow scarf for thirty years before it finally fell apart. Mantlepiece designs were made of strong coloured hard twine. I became skilful at this work and it helped to while away many a long weary day.

Our sports field in the centre of the compound was where many a future sports star in the G.A.A. learned perfection by daily practice and challenge games between selected teams. Here in the autumn, we organised sports (athletics), as well as hurling and football. The rivalry was intense and was based on county versus county, when possible. Boxing was another sport practised. This had a large following, myself included. Our promoters and teachers included Seán Mooney, Dublin; P. J. Ryan, Dublin; Jack Staunton, Ballina; and Denis O'Sullivan, Kerry. Our boxing stadium was the hut, its inmates our audience, our ring the concrete floor between the beds. Chess, too, had its devotees; some fine players we had. Liam Shortis, Ballybunion; and P. J. Ryan were the best in the whole camp. I can't of course forget the card players, and the pleasure we derived from it during many a wet dreary evening.

Jack Staunton was a fine young man, over six feet in height, and powerfully built. He was captured near the Tyrone border after a battle with the "Staters". Before that he had been a member of the R.I.C., and at the time of the Treaty was stationed at Dungannon barracks. The irony of his case was that shortly after the Treaty was signed, when Michael Collins was actively engaged in sending men and rifles to mount an offensive against the British in the occupied part of Ulster, contact was established with Jack Staunton. This resulted in the capture of Dungannon barracks, together with a considerable store of rifles, grenades and ammunition.

When Liam Lynch, Chief of Staff, was fatally wounded on the Knockmealdown mountains in April, the loss was a severe blow to us. I think that after his death de Valera decided it was better to hide all weapons held by the I.R.A. until some future day and order the remaining Republicans in arms to quietly disperse after doing so. In May, when de Valera and the Army

Executive ordered the cease-fire, it did not soften the rigours of our internment.

The exciting election of August, 1923, despite the triumphant show of success on the battlefield, did not yield the spectacular win expected by the Free State government. Dev escaped with his life when fired on at a public meeting in Ennis but was arrested and spent some months in jail. We were pleased in prison to learn that our party, Sinn Féin, returned well over forty T.D.s despite harassment and violence to our opponents by Oriel House (special detective force), who during the Civil War got an infamous name. Cheered up by the result and hopes that we'd rise again to reverse our recent failure in arms, we saluted our faithful friends outside who remained true to the ideal unitedly served, only a few years before, by eighty per cent of the people.

The months dragged along, slowly for us, though cheered from time to time by letters from home and an occasional food parcel. As autumn moved into winter it became apparent that releases were being considered by the 'Staters' as now they had nothing further to fear from armed action by our disorganised forces. Now it was common to hear the names of some of our prisoner friends being called each morning and notified of their release. This brought about a reduction of men in our camp but the releases were only a dribble until December. As Christmas approached the number of men released increased a good deal. Some still had to suffer on until the spring of 1924 before getting out.

It was no real surprise to me to hear one morning that I was free to leave. Together with some others we were brought into the office where our little money, confiscated on our internment, was handed back to us. We were then taken in a truck to Kildare Railway Station and each given a ticket to the nearest railway station to our homes. I arrived in Limerick in a confused state, partly due to being so many months separated from the public and especially from women, whose absence in our lives we missed. The loss of their influence and gentle manners in our daily lives was very much regretted. The rough usage of us by our captors had none of the humanity of the female species.

Coming into Limerick City en route to Devon Road Railway Station I wired home about my arrival. As my cash was scarce I ordered a cheap lunch at our old hostelry, "Hanratty's Hotel". Mrs. Hanratty, the well-known proprietor, was a staunch friend of ours and a personal friend of de Valera. That evening I met there Donncadh Ó Briain, later Fianna Fáil T.D., and a Mr. Warren from Abbeyfeale. Mr. Warren was no supporter of ours but strongly opposed to the I.R.A. Surprisingly, he greeted me with a hearty handshake, welcomed me home, and pulling some pound notes out of his pocket pressed me to accept them as a gift. Utterly confused at his generosity, I still had the necessary will power to refuse his gift, thanking him sincerely.

Arriving at Devon Road Station on the Tralee–Limerick Line, I was greeted by my wife and baby daughter, born while I was in prison and never of course seen by me until that night. Our old faithful workman, Jack Wrenn, drove them to the train to meet me. Stepping off the train I was greeted by a pipers' band (Meenahela), drawn up on the platform. In charge was an old friend, Stephen Barrett, with his brothers, Ned Barry and others.

Down the years I thought we might have achieved freedom, but sad is the tale—it was not to be realised. Here is farewell to the past I knew; may better days be ahead for our people and the land that we love.

APPENDIX

A HOSTAGE LOOKS BACK.

by Dr. Edward Harnett

In the spring of 1921 the tempo of the War of Independence had been stepped up and the British Forces, while feeling comparatively safe in their barracks behind steel-shuttered windows and barbed-wire entanglements, were not feeling so happy when they had to move out into open country when occasion demanded such ventures. So they had adopted the policy of taking hostages (or as they called them, "Mascots") with them as a sort of insurance against ambush by the I.R.A. That such tactics were not always productive of the results expected is now a matter of history.

Now in March of that year I was in medical practice in my native Abbeyfeale and one morning I was taken into custody by military and police and deposited in the police barrack in Newcastle West. At the same time the motorcycle I used in my work was dismantled and vital engine parts taken away and not returned to me until late December. In the barrack in Newcastle West I met two very nice lads—Willie Long of Feohanagh and Paddy Aherne of Dromcollogher—who were to be my companions for some time as hostages. We were introduced to our sleeping quarters, the dilapidated lock-up cell used for the temporary accommodation of drunks and bellicose tinkers. The only furniture was a ramshackle bed (double) for Long and Aherne and another (single) for me. We

---

Edward Harnett was Mossie Harnett's first cousin. This appendix is from a holograph in Edward Harnett's hand.

had straw mattresses and pillows and two or three army blankets. We had a meal and later in the evening we had tea.

The following morning I started on my new role of hostage. After a wash and shave in the barrack yard I had breakfast in the day room and then I was taken out to a lorry, handcuffed, and then chained to the tailgate. There was nothing to sit on. The lorry I was in was part of a convoy going to Limerick for stores and it had solid tyres. Now the roads in those days were very rough and full of potholes and the bumps and vibrations transmitted from the road up through the floor were unbearable if you chanced to stand on your heels, so I had to stand on tiptoe the whole way hanging on to some projection in the lorry. We drove into a big square of the military barrack in Limerick where great activity was going on with lorries and Crossley tenders continually moving in and out. A contingent of Auxiliaries pulled up beside the lorry I was in. They were cold and wet and in a vile humour. They had been out all night in a big round up in Clare, looking for Michael Brennan but with no success, and they consigned the elusive Pimpernel and all "Shinners" to the lowest pits of hell. Two of them catching sight of me came over and vented some more of their spleen on me. Luckily there was a Tommy on guard over me with a loaded rifle and I sensed that perhaps his presence kept them from going beyond verbal abuse. In any case I was quite glad to be ushered into the guardroom where there were six or seven Tommies who were quite friendly for the few hours I spent with them until we again took the road "home". Three or four times I was on the Limerick trip and the set-up was always the same.

In the Newcastle barrack we spent all our waking hours, when we were not on the road, in the day room where we had our meals, sometimes by ourselves and sometimes with the R.I.C. The food was quite good and we had no complaints on that score. And at night we could sit by the fire and when the Black and Tans were not around Long and Aherne, who had nice singing voices, used to render all the old favourites from "The Star of the County Down" to the West Clare Railway classic "Are you right there Michael, are you right?" The R.I.C. seemed to enjoy the impromptu concerts—their uniform might be British but perhaps their hearts were still a bit Irish. Sometimes we had amusing little incidents to relieve the monotony of life. One night leaving Limerick after dark our convoy halted between Adare and Croagh and an officer came back along the line from his car in front and as he passed my lorry shouted "Men keep your rifles well over the side, this is a very likely place for an ambush." Out went the rifles, but no sooner had he gone back to his car than in came the rifles and a young fellow shouted "The bloody old blighter has the wind up." There was general hilarity at this sally. Another little incident occurred one evening about dusk as a very sudden raid was made on a house near "Nolan's Heights", not far from Mossie Harnett's old home. Mossie at this time was Commandant of the number two Battalion West Limerick Brigade. Some of the chaps in the lorry were sent round to the back at the double and the search of the house and premises went on but nothing was found—contrary to expectations. At least the Tommies who raided from the front found nothing, but the lads at the back had better luck. Two of those who took their seats next to me were comparing notes—each had about a dozen nice brown eggs packed securely with hay in their haversack. As I had seen in the barrack in Limerick the hogwash they had for dinner I could not blame them for pinching a few eggs.

Now there was a young officer with whom I came into contact during my stay in Newcastle west. He was Captain Maunsell who had been badly wounded in Flanders and had been awarded the Military Cross for exceptional bravery in action. He was in charge of a party visiting the Kileedy district one evening, and it was the first time I was not handcuffed when out on these stunts. When they had some business completed round the area the whole party adjourned to the local pub and Maunsell took a Sergeant Major and myself into a little private snug where we spent an hour or two discussing matters in general but never touching dangerous ground. The

Captain was well educated, broadminded and easy to talk to. He never asked me any awkward or personal questions but he did say to me "Doctor, if you have any idea about attempting to escape, forget it—you will be shot. Keep cool and quiet and stay with me and you will be alright." I think the whole party were in a hilarious mood on the homeward journey, which was done in record time. It was good that evening to be able to use my hands freely and be able to put them in my pockets for cigarettes and matches.

Two days stand out in my memory. The first when I found myself before dawn on a bleak windswept crossroad a short distance from the village of Ballyhahill. Big forces of military, R.I.C., Black and Tans and Auxiliaries drawn from several barracks in West Limerick were engaged in a round-up of a wide circle of country with Ballyhahill in the centre. The Tommies on my lorry dismounted and planted a machine gun on a tripod in the middle of the crossroads. As the morning grew bright I could see troops in groups searching houses and driving people before them to the accompaniment of sporadic shooting. Soon a sizeable crowd had been herded on to the crossroad, men and boys from about sixteen to sixty years of age. A Black and Tan ordered them to form fours and a lot of shuffling went on but the formation was more sixes and sevens than fours. Then the Tan shouted "Come on you bastards, you knew damn well how to do it properly when you were being drilled in the hall the other night." The joker behind the machine gun waved the wicked muzzle from side to side in menacing fashion and the crowd was eventually manhandled into position and marched to the village. They were lined up outside the wall of the school and as my lorry pulled up opposite it I had a grandstand view of subsequent events.

The inquisition started with Head Constable Kearney from Newcastle as the chief inquisitor. Each individual was asked if he was drilling in the hall a few nights before and who was the drillmaster. Where there was any hesitation in answering or if the answer was in the negative the process of softening up was resorted to improve his memory and he was punched and battered against the wall by the Head Constable and his Black and Tan assistants. Then he was asked to shout aloud "God save the King and to Hell with de Valera and Sinn Féin." This was repeated all along the line and the unfortunate individual who refused this last test was subjected to further battering. It was a sickening scene of unbridled ferocity and savagery.

During my stay in Newcastle we noticed a definite coolness between the old R.I.C. members and the Black and Tans, two of whom—Collins and Smith, both motor drivers—were a really obnoxious combination. One night Collins tried to involve me in a discussion on ambushes and the mentality of people who saw preparations going on for such attacks and failed to give information to the Crown Forces. When I failed to fall in with his line of reasoning he got very worked up and brandishing his revolver he shouted "If there is a bloody ambush you'll be the first to go up." One of the Old R.I.C., Sergeant Gildea, a six-footer of commanding appearance, appeared to be in charge of the running of the barrack. He was supposed to have a reputation for manhandling people but we had nothing to say against him. He treated us very decently and kept the Tans in their place.

One evening the Tan driver, Smith, was at the wheel of a Crossley tender on a narrow little twisty road from the foot of Barna to Strand village and his driving was highly dangerous, cornering on two wheels and as often as not on the wrong side. Geese and hens along the road were scattered like chaff before the wind. Twice Gildea, who was sitting next to me behind Smith, warned him to take it easy but Smith only laughed and if anything increased his speed. Then Gildea went into action. Poking the barrel of his rifle into Smith's face he shouted, "You bloody madman, if you want to kill yourself you are not going to kill me—slow down or I'll put a bullet in your skull." Smith got the fright of his life and slowed immediately—all his arrogance and self-assurance gone like a burst bubble.

The second of the two days I remember so well was a day of tragedy. We three hostages were roused from our sleep at

4 a.m. and were escorted across the square to the military barrack. I was about to board a lorry when an officer said to a Tommy, "We only want two hostages today—take this chap back again to the police barrack and if he makes any attempt to escape shoot him." So with the Tommy's rifle at my back I crossed the square wondering if the safety catch was off. You see the night was very dark and if I or he happened to stumble the result might be disastrous, but I got to bed in safety. The following morning after breakfast Willie Long came in looking pale and shaking and he told me of the terrible tragedy he had witnessed. The lorry he was in that morning was parked on a road near Broadford and he saw military leaving a house a few hundred yards away. They had not gone very far when a young man named Boyce came out of the house, a horse's bridle swinging from his hand. He was apparently going to catch a horse to do some work and he was walking slowly across a field. A young soldier sitting next to Long rested his rifle on some part of the lorry and ran his eye along the sights. Long attached no importance to this as he thought the soldier was just practising sighting on a target. Now the Tommy whistled and the young man turned in the direction of the sound, and stopped. Immediately a shot rang out and Boyce fell— apparently dead. The Tommy walked over to the body, had a good look, then proceeded to pace the distance to the lorry. "Clean through the forehead at 220 paces—not bad shooting" was his comment and that was all he thought necessary to say about the cold blooded murder of a peaceful civilian. I daresay a mock inquiry was held and poor Boyce was adjudged to be an escaper from justice and shot in the act.

We had visitors to see us during our stay and my wife came in every other day. She was naturally very upset but was relieved to find me in good spirits. She was also delighted to see me in Abbeyfeale town on our expeditions there. We were now in our third week of enforced confinement and we were getting a bit 'browned-off' when word came to us from outside that we were to be interned—two in Ballykinlar and one in Spike Island. We took the news calmly enough, as it seemed that our present position at the mercy of Black and Tans was very precarious and fraught with great danger should an ambush take place. So we awaited the day of our departure. Then one morning I was having breakfast alone in the day room, Long and Aherne having gone out. The Head Constable said to me "You had better finish your breakfast quick as the lorry will be at the door for you in a few minutes so get your things packed. You are going away from here." I asked him where I was going to and all the information I got was that I was not coming back. I was ready at the door just as the lorry pulled up and Maunsell, who was in charge, shouted to me "Where are you going, Doctor, with the luggage?". When I explained he said "Well I am only going to Mount Brown and I'm coming back here this evening and I'm quite sure you are coming back with me." So into the day room again with my suitcase and as I passed the Head Constable I smiled. He scowled at me and if looks could have killed I should surely have died on the spot. So off I went to Mount Brown, a gentleman's residence a few miles from Rathkeale and which had been taken over by the troops. There was a large field or lawn in front of the house and a company of Infantry were doing advanced field drill and carrying out exercises in advancing and taking up positions under fire. The whole operation was carried out by whistle blasts—no oral commands were given and I was very interested in the whole proceedings. I had been looking on for about half an hour when Maunsell came over to me and invited me into the canteen and told me to wait for him there till he was ready to go. He also told me that I could have any refreshment I cared for. So I had a drink and some biscuits as I turned my attention to the action on the lawn. Maunsell had dispensed with handcuffs on this occasion, as once before, so I felt quite free and happy and when he returned to the canteen we got on the road again to Newcastle.

The next day was our last day as hostages. The day before the order for internment had been cancelled and we were informed that we were to be set free. Somewhere around 2 p.m. I was taken across the square to the military barrack where a senior officer read a little homily on law and order and finished up by telling me that if there were any more shooting or ambushes I would be held responsible and arrested again. I said to him that if such was the thinking on the matter it would be just as well for him to hold me as I could accept no responsibility for the peace of the country. He said no more but told me I was now free to go home. There was no suggestion of my giving any assurance or signing any documents about my future behaviour. And so I left him and was just in time to catch a train to Abbeyfeale and freedom. My stay with the Crown Forces had been a mixed grill—like the curate's egg—good in spots.

Looking back now after more than fifty years one of the disagreeable things I remember was the cold March winds as we speeded along the roads in open vehicles and the handcuffs which were very uncomfortable to say the least of it. And then there was the tension we were under on nights when we had gone to bed and we could listen to drunken Black and Tans expounding their ideas as to what should be done to all "Shinners" in their custody and another disagreeable thing was being exposed in the barrack square in Limerick to the unwelcome attention of Auxiliaries—probably the most select crowd of blackguards ever inflicted on our country.